D0386411

CROSSCURRENTS *Modern Critiques*

CROSSCURRENTS *Modern Critiques*
Harry T. Moore, *General Editor*

Morris Freedman

The Moral Impulse

MODERN DRAMA
FROM IBSEN TO THE PRESENT

WITH A PREFACE BY
Harry T. Moore

Carbondale and Edwardsville

SOUTHERN ILLINOIS UNIVERSITY PRESS

FEFFER & SIMONS, INC.

London and Amsterdam

N. H. TECH. INST.

PN
1851
.F7
1968

To Lionel Trilling

FIRST PUBLISHED, MARCH 1967
SECOND PRINTING, JUNE 1968

Copyright © 1967 by Southern Illinois University Press
All rights reserved
Library of Congress Catalog Card Number 67–10025
Printed in the United States of America
Designed by Andor Braun

THE MODERN THEATER has often been one of ideas, chiefly moral ideas. Morris Freedman in this book provides a fresh and thorough view of this theater and its concepts.

Mr. Freedman, Professor of English at the University of Maryland, is a man passionately interested in ideas, as his books, Confessions of a Conformist and Chaos in Our Colleges, forcefully demonstrate. And I well know, from a panel session at the University of New Mexico with Mr. Freedman and others, how vitally he can thrust ideas around in conversation.

His new book gets off to a running start, with a brisk discussion of Henrik Ibsen, and it breathlessly carries through to the type of drama that is dominant at the moment: the absurd. Mr. Freedman sees the latter as the lineal descendant of the moral impulse which characterized the drama of Ibsen, George Bernard Shaw, Anton Chekhov, and other earlier playwrights. For, as Mr. Freedman writes about these various authors, he continually keeps his eye on the development of the drama itself. His volume is therefore both a valuable treatment of separate playwrights and a lively survey of the modern theater.

The dramatists Mr. Freedman chooses to write about make an interesting group. Actually, he slights almost no important recent writer for the theater except perhaps Eugene O'Neill, to whom he doesn't devote a chapter although he refers to him from time to time. The inclusion of Oscar Wilde is rather startling, particularly to one who has recently seen the extremely popular 1965–66 (and probably '67) production of An Ideal Husband in London, with Richard Todd and Margaret Lockwood. The play seemed poor and thin in comparison with the contemporary performances of Shaw's You Never Can Tell (with Ralph Richardson), a comedy written only a year or so after Wilde's. One remembers that, on the opening night of Henry James's Guy Domville in 1895, the nervous author of that perhaps undeserved failure distracted himself by attending the performance of An Ideal Husband at another theater and found it "so helpless, so crude, so bad, so clumsy, feeble and vulgar" as to make him apprehensive about his own play, since the public seemed to relish the meretricious. An Ideal Husband hasn't improved with time, but today its acquired quaintness is an attraction and, of course, the current London production is in most respects first rate.

On the other hand, another of Wilde's comedies, The Importance of Being Earnest, is still alive, in every way a delightful farce. But the rest of Wilde's plays creak. Why, then, does Mr. Freedman give so much attention to this dramatist? He does so because Wilde marvelously lends himself to Mr. Freedman's study of the moral impulse as a dramatic force, and Mr. Freedman skillfully heightens his discussion of Wilde by including him in a chapter with Sean O'Casey, illustrating how neatly comparison often works in criticism; it is a technique which through parallels and contrasts brings out the distinct characteristics of individual authors. As Mr. Freedman says, after noting some of the critical objections to Wilde as a playwright: "A view of

Wilde in the company of O'Casey suggests an obscured moral dimension in Wilde; it may also help us
to see aspects of O'Casey in bolder perspective."

Further along, Mr. Freedman clarifies what his treatment of these two authors continually bears out:
"Wilde and O'Casey are not to be compared in terms
of their intention or their scope." O'Casey often reflects "the horror and the grotesque comedy of modern
gangsterism, a combination we find also in Brecht."
True; but what of Wilde? Mr. Freedman finds a dark
despair behind his glittering displays of wit. "But
Wilde is better than Maugham or Coward or Pinero
or Jones or Kaufman, all of whom write bright dialogue
or construct intricate plots, because there lurks in the
Wildean text a consciousness of the hellishness of all
the activity and talk."

Mr. Freedman of course expands this idea, but I
have quoted enough to indicate how unusual his treatment of such matters is. He is also fresh and perceptive
on Luigi Pirandello, Federico García Lorca, August
Strindberg, and other dramatists mentioned earlier in
this preface, as well as various recent American writers,
including Tennessee Williams and Edward Albee, and
also the European authors of the school of the absurd,
including Jean Genet and Samuel Beckett. I can at this
point only suggest again that Mr. Freedman provides
new insights into the works of all these writers and that
he continually gives us fresh perspectives on them.
This is a book on dramatic ideas which is itself full of
ideas and is also quite properly dramatic.

HARRY T. MOORE

Southern Illinois University
November 11, 1966

ACKNOWLEDGMENTS

MY GRATITUDE for help with this book extends back a number of years, to my wife particularly, and to my students, colleagues, friends, and teachers at CCNY, Columbia University, Queens College, and the University of New Mexico. For more recent editorial and critical aid, I am grateful to Miss Bess Earp. A large and general debt for an attitude of mind is but inadequately expressed in the dedication.

My thanks go also to the University of New Mexico for assistance to support work related to this study. In slightly different form, the chapter on Strindberg appeared in *Drama Survey*, Volume 2, Number 3 (February, 1963), 288–96; that on Wilde and O'Casey, in *College English*, Volume 25, Number 7 (April, 1964), 518–27, reprinted with the permission of the National Council of Teachers of English; and the chapters on Chekhov and Pirandello in *Modern Drama*, the first in Volume 5, Number 1 (May, 1962), 83–92, and the second in Volume 6, Number 4 (February, 1964), 368–77. I thank the editors for permission to use the material here.

Of course, all lapses in the work are my own.

MORRIS FREEDMAN

College Park, Maryland
September, 1966

CONTENTS

The Moral Impulse

MODERN DRAMA
FROM IBSEN TO THE PRESENT

1 THE MORALITY OF PARADOX: IBSEN'S SOCIAL PLAYS

IN WHAT is usually considered the middle of his career, Ibsen wrote three plays, one hard upon the other: *Ghosts* (1881), *An Enemy of the People* (1882), and *The Wild Duck* (1884). *Ghosts* has commonly been taken as Ibsen's response to the criticism of *A Doll's House* (1879); *An Enemy of the People*, to the criticism of *Ghosts*; and *The Wild Duck*, as Ibsen's distressed dismissal of the excessively idealistic "Ibsenites" who had sprung up to defend him against the criticism provoked by the earlier plays.

History aside, the three plays offer a unified study of the interaction between ideas and the persons who embody them in certain circumstances. If there is any simple "social" intention in these plays, as well as in *A Doll's House*, which set the trilogy into motion but is simpler in conception and execution, and *Hedda Gabler* (1890), which followed the trilogy after an interval and is a further complication and refinement of its social intention, it is that no social situation has a meaning that can be totally separated from the whimsical, undetermined, particularized characters of the persons caught up in it.

In spite of much appearance to the contrary, Ibsen was rarely a simple polemicist. Indeed, Shaw himself, in *The Quintessence of Ibsenism*, recognized this in his elaborate symbolic analyses of the early and late plays; it is surprising how much he limits himself to surface appearance in the middle plays. Ibsen himself, as Shaw acknowledged, insisted that he was a poet, and that he should be taken at his word: he insisted, that is, that his text spoke for him: "What I have said I have said." The more Ibsen achieved his esthetic intention, the more lost the pure motivating "idea" or thesis became. Thus, his plays are rarely what they appear to be; indeed, they may often be exactly *not* what appears plain, on the surface. As in the work of all poets, Ibsen's meanings, not least in the "social" plays, may be found in paradox, in the tensions between appearances and depths.

Let us consider, but for a moment only, the character of Nora Helmer, perhaps the best-known and one of the most appealing of Ibsen's women. Is she blameless for the unrest and crisis that develop in her doll's house? Scarcely. Either she lives according to the notions of courtly love, expecting her husband to risk himself in rescuing her from the dragons of law and society, or she lives according to the latest and shallowest notion of emancipated womanhood, abandoning her family to go out into the world in search of "her true identity." She is troubled by her husband's passion for her as a woman; most of the time she sees herself as a chaste doll, worshipped from afar, or as a medieval maiden waiting to be rescued. Of course, Helmer plays to her wishes, perhaps even implants them, but when the time comes to drop the playing, Helmer is ready, Nora is not: she simply assumes another role, that of the wronged but now "enlightened" woman. (In discussion of the womanly woman, Shaw takes up the matter of role-playing, but with only the most oblique reference to Nora Helmer.)

In *Ghosts*, the larger meaning depends on what we

make of Mrs. Alving, who is at the heart of the play's paradox. If we take *Ghosts* simply as Ibsen's polemical answer to the criticism of *A Doll's House,* then the line we are to follow with Mrs. Alving from the beginning is sympathetic. This is what happens when a wife does *not* leave her husband. But clearly Mrs. Alving is not to be extensively compared with Nora Helmer, or Captain Alving with Mr. Helmer. Mrs. Alving is a woman whose respect for intellectual formulation is so great that she absorbs what passes for ideas whole. In her respect for thought, or the appearance of thought, she suppresses spontaneous feeling. She is always conscious of social demand, whether she acquiesces to it, or whether she flaunts it. She marries Alving without love (for which, perhaps, she is not to be wholly blamed); she is attracted by the fool Manders, who simply shines with "moral" ideas; she is ready, partly as the result of her newfound, "liberating" intellectuality, to countenance a liaison between Oswald and his half-sister. She is shocked into genuine feeling by traumatic scenes only: Oswald making love to Regina; Oswald going mad.

In spite of her intellectual pretenses, she has allowed her life to be guided by a particularly shallow rule: not merely to be faithful to her "awful" husband (although she did try once to escape through an affair) but to keep up appearances. Her main activity for twenty years has been to act in a kind of morality drama, written by her and Manders, or rather, by her alone, for poor Manders does not often know what is happening on the stage which Mrs. Alving always tries to control. And it is only when this stage becomes occupied by another person, when Oswald comes home, do we, the larger audience, begin to see the drama behind the drama that Manders saw, behind the simple one of the wronged wife, which would have been the answer to the critics of A *Doll's House* (and Ibsen's answer to a Pastor Manders). Oswald's presence makes us suspect—late in the superficial drama, but at the beginning of the actual one—that Mrs. Alving's picture of her husband is perhaps distorted. We wonder about the two versions she offers of Captain Alving, one to Pastor Manders (the man she wanted as lover), the other to her son. We suspect the immaculateness of her lifelong motivation. For how else than he did, we suddenly wonder, could Captain Alving, a man apparently of high spirits and vitality and emotional capacity, have behaved with this sort of woman? What sort of rapport could he have had with the shrivelled, unfulfilled person that Mrs. Alving seems to be? How could the woman who loves Pastor Manders—only an idea of a man—have also properly loved a full-blooded man? And where else could Alving have found his pleasures—imprisoned as he was— but in his home, in drinking, in idle reading, and in making love to the maid? We must pause to speculate about what sort of morbid satisfaction Mrs. Alving may have derived from suppressing the captain's "joy of life," which she describes so candidly to Oswald.

Mrs. Alving's tragedy, then has little to do with the play's rebuttal to A *Doll's House.* The tragedy of Mrs. Alving results from her incapacity to accommodate to circumstance, from her incapacity to accept genuine feeling, from her need to live by ideas, however simple, inadequate, and inappropriate.

We are surely intended to sympathize with Mrs. Alving, and we do. As much as Oedipus, she is the victim of her own pride as well as of circumstances beyond her comprehension and control. She is the new woman not quite fully formed, not quite in full command, and the gulf between what she might be, what she thinks she is—managing her husband's affairs, reading the latest books, playing with the notion of a liaison with Manders, "sophisticated" enough to accept incest—and what she actually is, groping for definition and identity, is the abyss into which she plunges. She is not simply an innocent, passive victim of Manders' foolish and interfering advice, a Nora Helmer thrust back into domestic travail; like any tragic hero, Mrs. Alving substantially makes her own fate. Whatever Ibsen might have begun with, he produces a drama whose complexity is rooted below surface thesis.

Francis Fergusson has compared *Ghosts* with *Oedipus* in its structure: we are introduced to the action shortly before the climax; the drama is built on a large past. We may find a number of other interesting parallels between Sophocles and Ibsen in addition to the dramaturgic one. Laius and Captain Alving both hover over the action; although never seen, they are important characters. The pressures of society determine both Oedipus and Mrs. Alving in much of what they do; indeed both plays require us to understand how much force society and its gods can exert on the individual. It is his social responsibility which compels King Oedipus into uncovering his abominable past; it is a sense of social responsibility which impels Mrs. Alving to go through with her charade of proper domesticity. But we expect Mrs. Alving to do better than Oedipus; she does not, after all, have quite the same occasion for tragedy as Oedipus had. She has no adequate compulsion to let one action lead to another to compound evil. She is not so totally a victim of fate, and the play achieves much of its impact through this paradox. She is the victim more of herself than of any gods.

It is with *Lear*, and with *Oedipus* in its largest dimension, man's relation to his own nature, that

Ghosts has a critical connection. Mrs. Alving, like Lear, may be seen as trying, however feebly by comparison, to make some order for herself out of chaos. Like Lear, she stages situations; like Lear, she keeps being outraged. Her world is dominated by disease (syphilis), catastrophe (the orphanage fire), and morally ambiguous decisions (incest and mercy killing). Her strength (as evidenced by her control of her family arrangement), her "intellect" (those advanced books Manders riffles), her capacity for truth (the confession to Oswald of what kind of man Captain Alving really was) help her in no way against the immense arbitrariness of the universe. As with Lear, all her expectations, the large ones and the trifling ones, are shattered. We are not present, of course, to see her accept her moral limitations, humbled, resigned, as we do see Lear. We see her, as we see Oedipus, ready to tear out her eyes over the horror developing on the stage.

Hedda Gabler is the reverse of Mrs. Alving. Where Mrs. Alving allows herself to be moved by the people around her and is affected by them and, in turn, uses them as a rationale for the extremity of her situation, Hedda Gabler manages to a considerable degree to control her environment. Hedda manipulates the world in the manner of a military strategist concerned with long-range possibilities, perhaps a talent she had gotten from her father, the general, as she had inherited his pistols from him. This may be bad, always reordering experience, setting the background, staging scenes and whole acts, not allowing reality to take its whimsical, arbitrary way. Staging gets sticky, as Pirandello will show us, and carries its own risks. But consider that Hedda's attempt to control the world springs from her feeling of strength and independence, from her vitality, from her impulse to make things better for herself. She is simply trapped by the limited possibilities: Løvborg might have turned out like Alving; Judge Brack is a blackmailing brute. These are Hedda's alternatives to Tesman. Her tragedy is that, like Candida, she marries a weak man. Unlike Candida and Mrs. Alving, however, she is not accommodating. She will not be a mother to Tesman. Like Candida, she is not intellectual, and unlike Mrs. Alving, she will not fool herself into thinking she is; yet she desperately needs a way of independent fullfilment consonant with her character. She manipulates lives.

Hedda Gabler is compulsive, excessively so, in her editing of the text given to her; she accepts nothing, not even the furniture or the lighting of a room she is in. The only men available to whom she can respond seriously are Brack and Løvborg. And her tragedy, at last, is that she is so much more woman than Nora Helmer (who did marry a Brack) or Mrs. Alving (who married a Løvborg). Doomed to remain with Tesman, incapable of submitting to Brack, frustrated in her shaping of Løvborg, she exercises her option to get out of life, a life that has defeated her, as it has Mrs. Alving, in big and little things.

Paradox, too, is at the heart of *An Enemy of the People*. To oversimplify, we have a good honest man involved in a good honest project which he destroys because of his very goodness and honesty. It seems to me a serious limitation, however, to read the play only as a tract. Dr. Stockmann is not just a hero standing for justice, self-sacrifice, courage in the face of tyranny. He is certainly this, but he is also a very human, very confused man, who turns heroism into farce, who, more than any villain in the play, destroys his own cause. His character is highly particularized; he is no stock idealist. His motivation, for example, is a complicated mechanism, involving his relation to authority and, specifically, to his older and more important brother, his need for adulation, his extravagant generosity. Consider the embarrassing scene in which the doctor toys like a child with the symbols of the mayor's authority.

Opposed to Dr. Stockmann we have a bad dishonest man, who, we recognize, could bring the good, necessary project into being because of his very badness. Peter Stockmann's sense of political exigency, his Machiavellian instinct for reality, his ability to manipulate people to his ends, his hypocrisy, his shiftiness, his close management of everyday small and large affairs, make him ideal to be, if he wishes, the true friend of the people.

An Enemy of the People goes a step beyond *Ghosts*. Ideas by themselves, however noble and essential, cannot be expected to make their way by their own force. If ideas can destroy, as in *Ghosts*, they can also be destroyed. The whole town may become sick from the organisms in the water supply, lose its attraction as a tourist center, harm itself irrevocably, because Dr. Stockmann's revelations were not presented in terms of the realities of the moment. It requires a conscious misreading of the text, almost as flagrant as the townspeople's willful refusal to see the consequences of the polluted water, to be taken in entirely by Dr. Stockmann. His megalomanic anticipation of praise, his refusal to consider any alternatives to his solution of the problem, the very privacy of his research render suspect the altruism of his motives and even of his findings. (The doctor may well be right in his conclusions, but how can we trust him altogether once we know him? What "controls" were there for his "research"? What other hypotheses might account for the organisms? What other way than his might the pollution be handled?) Any crackpot may come up at some time with a genuine marvel of one sort or another, but it is asking too much of society not to be skeptical. Dr. Stockmann may well be right in his gloomy predictions of doom for the town, but the town may be right also in not promptly acclaiming him its savior.

We are not given any attractive alternative to Dr. Stockmann. If the doctor is a frivolous, sophomoric fool, his brother, the mayor, is a pompous, stuffy one. The several groups of townsfolk are cynically depicted as opportunistic, unstable, shallow. But it is not the mayor who is disappointed in the character of his constituents; it is the doctor who overestimates and idealizes his supporters, attributing enlightenment, courage, and intelligence to them. Perhaps all public servants should be like the brave, dedicated physician, and we are sure that citizens should be everything the doctor originally thinks of them as being. But it is wrong to condemn the citizens for turning out to be no more than what the mayor knew them to be all along, or to condemn the mayor for working within the narrow limits of political sophistication rather than within the broader ones of political naïveté.

We are close to having a misanthropic work on our hands if we must conclude that nobility and courage can be corrupted by innocence, if we conclude that everyone in the town is a villain or a fool. (The episode in which Morten Kiil, Dr. Stockmann's father-in-law, accuses Dr. Stockmann himself of venality is Swiftian in its sudden opening up of the pit of human ugliness.) If we develop any doubts about the doctor's findings and recommendations, we must also have them about the hypocrisy of the mayor. Our affection for the doctor is no reason for accepting without hesitation everything he says; our disaffection from the mayor is no reason for rejecting everything *he* says. We are at an impasse.

Only detachment, coolness, absence of commitment can now help us, and only one man, an outsider, displays these qualities, Captain Horster. The sea captain, of course, comes off no better than the doctor at the hands of the townspeople. But his willingness to judge fairly, to give the doctor a chance to be heard, are in and of themselves moral qualities. The town may indeed be doomed, for at the point where the captain appears to support Dr. Stockmann it is beyond being helped effectively by either the doctor or the mayor. Both have been carried beyond the operation of reason to gestures of faith and of mindless affirmation. The two brothers, both self-professed public servants, have worked themselves into passions which can no longer serve anyone, not even themselves; the captain, aloof and dispassionate, not even a rooted member of the community, alone holds for a moment the possibility of redemption for the town.

We are dizzied by the concentric circles of ironies: the doctor may or may not be right, but he cannot be listened to; the mayor may be corrupt, but he may not be altogether wrong in his opposition to his brother; the townspeople (much like the citizens in Shakespeare's Roman plays) scarcely deserve, in any event, all the concern lavished on them. Truth and need, the public good and the private lust, all get stirred together. Nobility becomes the victim of personality. Even if the town never suffers from any microorganisms, it has already been sickened and debilitated by its treatment of the doctor. Morally it is already diseased. In *Ghosts*, the inadequacy of a vessel to the ideas it contains causes individual tragedy; in *An Enemy of the People*, the incapacity of ideas to accommodate to the unyielding demands of person, time, and place causes social disaster.

The Wild Duck brings together themes from *Ghosts* and *An Enemy of the People*. Just as certain scenes in *Ghosts* are dominated by the ghost of Captain Alving, so certain ones in *The Wild Duck* are by the late Mrs. Werle. Her presence hangs as heavily over Werle and Gregers as Alving's does over his wife and son. In both plays, the master's illicit relation with a servant has resulted in the birth of a daughter. In both, much is made of the passing on of hereditary afflictions.

The thematic relation with *An Enemy of the People*, however, seems more important. Gregers is Dr. Stockmann uprooted, free-floating, detached from family and even from a worthy cause. Where Dr. Stockmann at least had the interests of a town in mind on the very particular issue of water pollution, the only issue that impels Gregers is the abstract one of "the demands of the ideal." Gregers is a grotesque development of Dr. Stockmann. Dr. Stockmann shouts out: "What does the destruction of a community matter, if it lives on lies! It ought to be razed to the ground, I tell you! All who live by lies ought to be exterminated like vermin!" Gregers echoes him when he describes Hialmar as building his home upon a lie. Both Gregers and Dr. Stockmann have lived too long away from civilization and its realities; they both return from cold exile in the north.

It is one thing to make an assertion like Dr. Stockmann's about living by lies, which applies to a whole society, and which may well have validity in a large context, but it is another to undermine systematically a weak and foolish individual's small arrangement of reality to suit himself. The doctor hurls himself against the wall of society and is thrown back; he himself is finally injured. If the town is in any way hurt, it is only indirectly the doctor's responsibility, if it is his at all, for not finding a way of effectively communicating his message. But the death of Hedvig is explicitly to be assigned to Gregers. Stockmann's fanatical devotion to truth regardless of circumstances becomes in Gregers a service in the interests of death. It is opposed to life with all of its compromises and lies; it can only accept the sharp, uncompromising absoluteness of the ideal, of death, which is perfect. The funereal Gregers wants it understood that suicide is to be his own fate.

The dim-witted, smug, unrelenting, ugly self-righteousness of Gregers serves the poisonous ends of fanaticism. Yet even Gregers, like Dr. Stockmann, is fanatical in a noble cause. We cannot deny the abstract validity of his wishing to have persons live by the truth. It is certainly better to live by truths and ideals than by illusions, for deceptions and hypocrisies to be wiped away, for Nora to be given her due as a person, for Mrs. Alving to be able to break away from her unsavory past, for the townspeople to heed Dr. Stockmann. But it is ignorant or stupid to behave as though the truth always will or must have easy, immediate acceptance. There are large truths and small ones, there is the right time to reveal the truth, and the wrong time, the right place and the wrong one. This simple enough distinction, obvious to Relling, to Gina, to Werle, is in no way apparent to the high-mindedly dense Gregers. The earthy Relling and the airy Gregers argue the point abstractly, but philosophical matters easily enough become practical ones. Hedvig, the child, grimly acts out Greger's murky symbolic nonsense.

The Wild Duck is filled with hints of plots, of relationships, of character transformations, which throb all around the main business. Relling is apparently interested in Mrs. Sorby, but she will have nothing seriously to do with him. He is frivolous. A man of possibly greater innate worth than Werle, he will not, as Werle did, subdue and put to work his various energies. He succumbs to his bitterness. As for Werle himself, the question of his "treatment" of his wife and of Ekdal is left unanswered. That, as Werle indicates with a wave of the hand, was the past, and all of his son's accusations and innuendoes are irrelevant to the present. The world has gone on, changes have occurred. The Werle of today is not the Werle of yesterday. Today Werle does right by Ekdal (and more than right, for Ekdal's empty-headed foolishness suggests that Werle's account of Ekdal's imprisonment may be accurate), and is ready to do right by his son. Werle behaves with full generosity toward Hedvig, too, who may or may not be his daughter. He behaves with more good sense and kindness than Hialmar, who, natural father or not, has been the day-to-day father of the girl, and who, under the compulsion of Gregers, acts toward her with flighty and ultimately dangerous disregard.

Ibsen's sardonic humor emphasizes the folly of all the busy righteousness and smartness. Look whom Gregers is trying to redeem! Hialmar is a ninny, a clown, a good-hearted, good-natured, good-looking, self-indulgent, simple-minded lout. He cannot even run away from home like any self-respecting ten year old. Gregers goes about presenting the claim of the ideal to humanity and cannot keep clean his own room. But Ibsen's wryest humor is to be found in some of the pretentious symbolism about the wild duck. Only the weak-minded, the unbalanced, or the young get carried away by the symbolic solemnity, Gregers, Hedvig, Hialmar, Ekdal. The wild duck is another red herring. We can make so much of it that finally we make nothing. The serious persons in the play never get involved with equating the duck with

Hedvig, with Hialmar, with Ekdal; they impatiently dismiss this kind of poeticizing. Watch the birdie and miss the sleight of hand, miss the study of depravity in the name of morality. As in *An Enemy of the People,* we can get so involved in the mechanics of the events, we neglect the character of the persons involved in them. And, of course, in all of these plays, it is so much easier, intellectually and morally, to study the surface scrupulously.

But the duck does lurk as an obvious enough symbol, and we cannot entirely pretend that it is only a red herring. Even before we learn of the duck, Werle refers to Ekdal in terms of the duck. "There are people in the world," he says to his son, "who dive to the bottom the moment they get a couple of slugs in their body and never come to the surface again." Gregers is taken by the image, for, when he learns of the duck, he promptly equates it with Hialmar and then calls himself a bird dog who will raise the duck from the depths. This wry, point-by-point working out of the allegorical intent might have remained simple burlesque, an instance of how literary obsession can unsettle the weak mind, were it not for the climax that actually develops, Hedvig's self-identity with the duck under Gregers' relentless pressure. The glib symbolism of the duck would remain farcical did it not result in death.

A good deal is made of the freedom, the wildness, of the duck before its capture. These paeans to the untrammeled natural state of the duck are ironic. Man, unlike the duck, does not live in nature. He must always be trapped by the limitations of native capacity, the demands of society, the accidents of fate. Moreover, he must, when necessary, actively, consciously, imprison himself by life illusions, as Relling puts it. The wild duck in its attic prison prospers and gets fat, and it would have continued doing so (as would Hialmar and Hedvig) if Gregers had not insisted on imposing the ideal on the real, imposing literature on life. In addition to the afflictions Relling catalogues Gregers as suffering from, Gregers would seem to have an acute case of literature.

The tragicomedy of the duck is in the tradition of the grotesque, macabre comedy we find in *Lear*, in Dostoyevsky, in Kafka. It is chillingly, terrifyingly funny to find a forest in an attic which sends out a literary miasma to poison the residents of an ordinary flat. Every time the little symbolic world of Gregers comes up against the practical one of Gina we have a joke. Gregers says at one point: "For my part, I don't thrive in marsh vapors," referring to the secret of Gina's past. "Goodness knows," exclaims Gina, "there's no vapors in this house, Mr. Werle; I give the place a good airing every blessed day." Later in the conversation, it suddenly strikes her as especially unfair for Gregers to complain about vapors when he has made such a vaporous mess in his room. Hialmar, too, of course, is literary about everything, as Relling points out. "How could you help writhing with penitence and remorse?" Hialmar asks Gina when he discovers her past. "Oh, my dear Ekdal," answers Gina, "I've had all I could do to look after the house and get through the day's work." Life, it is clear, can only be demeaned and parodied by literature. As for Hialmar, he will do a good deal of such writhing.

In *The Wild Duck* the social context is irrelevant. But even in the earlier plays, for all of the force exerted by society on lives, individuals are not absolved of their own complicity in their fate. The sins of the fathers may indeed be passed on to the children, but the disaster that ensues is not automatic, and certainly not to be blamed on society; the tragedy is personal.

This is made peculiarly explicit in *The Wild Duck*, for Gregers is to be found guilty for Hedvig's death, not Werle for her weak eyes. The question of heredity itself, present in both *Ghosts* and *The Wild Duck* and alluded to lightly in *A Doll's House*, also takes the issue of responsibility out of the social context and places it into a personal or, at least, a "natural" one. As in Henry James, another great literary admirer of Ibsen, moral issues in Ibsen, whatever their roots, whatever their genesis, are ultimately resolved among persons.

Ibsen's final paradox may be found in the covering over of the moral depths of his plays by their striking social surface. Society, for all of its contributing energy, is not so responsible as an individual himself for tragedy, for failure to fulfill promise, for man's indifference to man, and most of all, for the general human incapacity to resist or change social demand. Ibsen's heroes, and they are few, are those who can live not only with themselves and with others but in society and with fate. They are, most importantly, concerned with the largest possibility, not with truth alone, but with lies and deceptions and accommodations, with compromises and resignations, with the whole range of human effort to live in the daily, natural, and human world.

We cannot neglect the moral thrust of the device of hereditary disease. Like Zola, Ibsen insists on a continuity of responsibility, from generation to generation. But this responsibility we must always set into the larger context of a total social and personal reality. In this sense, Ibsen may be called a realist but not simply because he recorded what the camera might see; he was a realist because he sensed and could realize invisible potential; the reality of human promise is a moral and imagined reality: this was Shaw's reality, too.

2 STRINDBERG'S POSITIVE NIHILISM

STRINDBERG, like Ibsen, presents a surface of thesis. *The Father* appears to be a play in answer to Ibsen's "woman love." It is apparently based on woman hate and ostensibly depicts the systematic destruction by a wife of her husband. The text even contains a specific reference to *Ghosts*, in which a good word is said for Captain Alving. *Miss Julie,* although its thesis is less obvious than that of *The Father*, depicts the destruction of a "decadent" member of the aristocracy by a rising member of the lower classes. This conflict is complicated by the forces of feminine emancipation which have made Miss Julie so uncertain of her character. (Miss Julie, like Hedda Gabler, the product of the new enlightenment, cannot shape her world to suit her romantic dreams and so leaves it. Unlike Hedda, however, she has so lost possession of herself, she begs to be ordered to kill herself.)

But Strindberg's thematic surface, far more obviously than Ibsen's, pulsates with disturbances that have their energy in an undertow of passion, with shocks and heavings that are generated before our eyes. Strindberg's drama is dynamically psychological. Tones, atmospheres, characters, moods change as we watch; logic and predictability, order, coherence give way before the effects of desperate needs and of violent whim; they become lost in the chaos and depths of the mental landscape.

In *The Father* we see an inflexible, principled man degenerate inexorably to a whimpering infantilism. The captain insists that it is he alone who will decide the education of his daughter; he rejects the compromise offered by his wife, which would allow the daughter to vote on her future, even though the compromise would favor his position. At his strongest, at his most assertive, we can glimpse signs of the captain's weakness; his descent to a whining dependence, to a literal swaddling by the nurse who handled him as a baby, is much less the result of his wife's attack on him than it is of his own softness of character and will, emerging at last to the determining surface. We learn very early that the captain has allowed himself to be dominated by a ménage of whimsical, willful, superstitious, fanatical women; his brother-in-law, Laura's brother, has foisted off on him at least one of them and considers it something of a joke. It was as a mother to him, both the husband and the wife agree, that the wife married him. Like a child seeking relief from some arbitrary, even terrible parental imposition, the captain implores his wife to release him from the doubt of his paternity of Bertha, but, like a child who lives under some primal taboo that is superior to his own will, the captain is actually unable to allow himself to be so released. Nor of course can he ever logically be released, for, as he points out, in a mad scene echoing Lear and Dostoyevskeyan tableaus, what father can ever be certain of his child, what father can ever be other than putative, a lament that, horrible as it may suddenly seem, is only of the nature of things (short of chastity belts): as well lament the unrelenting pull of gravity.

If the captain acts out of an absurd logic, compelled

step by step in a scheme of things which seems to have an order (he is the father, he has the right to make decisions regarding his daughter; he doubts his father-hood, which is to say his masculinity and his maturity; his ceases to decide and to act; he returns to infancy and, back farther still, to death), Laura acts out of an illogical instinct which has its own order and inevitability. Incapable of any but the most simple strategy, without detail or preliminary planning, a strategy shaped only by the dimmest notion of distant victory, Laura is capable of the most refined, most carefully exercised tactical skill. It is the captain, after all, who first brings up the theme of the universal uncertainty of fatherhood; it is the doctor who first suggests the possibility of certifying the captain's insanity. She immediately assimilates the implicit possibilities; at once they become measures in her campaign. Yet it would be an error to consider her heartless, unaware of the nature of her behavior, indifferent to its appearance.

LAURA   But I didn't mean this to happen. I never really thought it out. I may have had some vague desire to get rid of you—you were in my way—and perhaps, if you see some plan in my actions, there was one, but I was unconscious of it. I have never given a thought to my actions—they simply ran along the rails you laid down. My conscience is clear, and before God I feel innocent, even if I'm not. You weighed me down like a stone, pressing and pressing till my heart tried to shake off its intolerable burden. That's how it's been, and if without meaning to I have brought you to this, I ask your forgiveness.

Even here, her sensitivity to the implications of things is evident. This poignant, strainingly honest, unsparing self-analysis is part of her capacious tactical instinct; she does not justify herself, that is to say, she does not find a rationale or a justification to philosophize her action, she merely describes herself. Her intentions are perhaps those of a predatory animal, of the female spider, but she lives with them, exercises them, in the cause of what she is sure is a worthy endeavor, the protection of the maternal prerogatives.

It is plain that in the background of the elemental, sexual struggle between the father and mother is the issue of the emergence of woman as an individual. Strindberg may sneer at Ibsen's idolatry of woman, he may suggest that woman needs no more rights than those she already possesses in abundance (witness Laura who, as a plain matter of fact, regardless of law, states that she is the stronger of the two, rather disarming the captain), but it is the background of Laura's ignorance, the legal dispossession of her rights, which triggers the developing explosion. The captain will not talk out his differences with his wife, answering her suggestion for a compromise by pointing out, with an adolescent preciseness, that the halfway point between the town and their residence is the railroad station. The captain does not trouble to inform his wife of the details or significance of his meteoritic studies, and while her confusion of a microscope with a spectroscope might have been willful, part of her campaign to have him certified as insane, it might equally well have been the result of ignorance. Nor can we blame her without extenuation for the interception of her husband's orders for books, unless we are ready to accept the captain's attitude that his meteoritic researches were none of her business, that these, essentially, preceded the whole family's welfare. All Laura can see is that the captain does not read or use all of the books he orders (common enough if one knows scholars) and that the household expenses are being squeezed. (This is especially ironic, for the captain keeps the household books, doling out expense money.)

Miss Julie, too, while it may have its roots in social questions, rises to the more airy atmosphere of psychology. Miss Julie's fate is as much the result of encountering a representative of the new proletariat and of her mother's "enlightened" upbringing as it is of her own particularity of character, her uncertainty of identity, her playfulness with passion, her alternate arrogance and submissiveness, her extravagant romanticism, her plain compulsion to perversity. Hating sex, she submits to Jean; hating men and wishing pathologically to humble them, she asks Jean to command her to suicide.

The Father gets starker and starker as it proceeds. Its movement is a steady one, an intensification at a fixed rate toward the sheer monotone of the finale. Modulation is negligible. *Miss Julie* is a chiaroscuro of tones. Before the union, there is gallantry in the air, the colors of emotion, summer perfumes, but with patterns of sudden blackness: the gentle flirtatiousness of Julie and Jean and the momentary flashes of viciousness and selfishness. After, there is dullness and greyness and the distortions and blurrings of romance (Lake Como with its incessant rains and quarrelling couples), the interplay of the changing affections of Julie and Jean toward each other, Julie's bleakness in her frustration and degradation and the red violence of her fury. Miss Julie is playing on the fringes of actuality, laughing at the depths that surround her; we are present as she totters erratically but certainly, toward the plunge. Oppressed by will, dominated by it, she has not even the passing satisfaction of Hedda Gabler's independence, of Hedda's modest moment of control of fate (the puppetry of Lovborg), and she retains only enough will in the end to ask that Jean exercise will for her.

Miss Julie and *The Father* show characters as they move steadily toward failure and death. In *Easter* we see a man moving upward toward some degree of self-understanding and success as a person. Elis is a figure almost as obnoxious as the black Gregers in *The Wild Duck*. He is brimming with an aggressive self-pity, with pride, with a coldness of soul that excludes the rest of the universe. He is solipsistic, taking every event in his neighborhood as having a meaning only for him. (Once when the telephone rings, he hears his own voice answering.) He has been chosen, as he sees it, for endless punishment. He rises out of his pit as the result, first, of the effects on him of his fiancée, Kristina, and of his mother, who are real enough persons, but also as the result of the workings on him of his sister, Eleanora, and of the debtor, Lindkvist, who are more than real, other than real, and represent forces as well as themselves.

Kristina works on Elis by following her bent, humoring him only just so far, letting him live with his jealousy and then with the truth. She opposes his volatility with calmness. His mother resists him openly and logically. "Your coldness," she says to him about his attitude toward Kristina, "freezes her heart." When he petulantly laments the family's fate for the hundredth time, "but why do we who are innocent suffer for his fault?" evoking the ancient dilemma of original sin, his mother dismisses him impatiently, "Oh, be quiet!" It is the mother who establishes plainly the way of redemption, the change necessary in Elis for his "punishment" to cease. "Men are human," she says, "and one must take them as they are." She says about Eleanora, "Sane or not, for me she is wise—for she knows how to bear life's burdens better than I do, better than any of us."

Eleanora, too, makes explicit the need for patience, forebearance, acceptance, self-denial. "Stop judging people," she tells Benjamin, "even those who are convicted of sin." But her effect is in her example. Even Elis sees this. "Poor Eleanora," he mutters at the end of Act I, "she's so unhappy herself, and yet she can make others happy." Her endless sweetness and gentleness, her flights of fancy (listening to the birds and to the telephone wires), her other-worldly disregard for the legal amenities of this world make it possible for her to see and state arrangements invisible and impossible to the others. She comes as close as anyone to stating the theme of the play, "Everyone has to suffer today, Good Friday, so as to remember Christ's suffering on the cross," and, indeed, at one moment or another, every one of the principal characters identifies himself with Christ.

But Elis's "sufferings"—about the family's debt to the creditor, about the failure of his student in his examination, about the rejection of him by another student, about his mother's and sister's insanity, about his father's guilt—are all external and theatrically masochistic. He flaunts his wounds and his pride in them. It is necessary for him really to suffer, to pass through agonies of character, to be redeemed. And it is here that Lindkvist plays his role. A much imposed on creditor, he comes to forgive, to offer mercy, not the coldness and heartlessness of justice, which Elis insists on. Almost an allegorical figure, he throws his huge shadow over the players; he knows what they have been talking about when he was away; he can, *deus-ex-machina* like, manipulate the plot, bringing up an encounter with Elis's father that predated the swindling. He has the joviality, the comical quality (those galoshes that squish all through his scenes), but also the supernatural tone of a Santa Claus figure, which he is. He comes to bring salvation to the family at the expense of Elis's humiliation. Elis's pride must break; he must write to the student who rejected him;

he must meet the governor to whom he objects so vehemently. "We're all human," Lindkvist tells him, "and in life's crises we must take one another as we are with all our faults and weaknesses—swallow each other neck and crop. Go to the Governor!"

Both Eleanora and Lindkvist represent extremes of accommodation. Eleanora works with instinct and heart; Lindkvist with logic, head, and a sense of character. They are inner and outer forces, and they meet just before the end of the play, just after Lindkvist has laid down the procedure for Elis's saving of the family, and join. Lindkvist may be able to lay down the rules for Elis's salvation, but it is Eleanora who will see to it that they are put into effect.

Easter modulates the harshness of *Miss Julie* and *The Father*. Elis is like the captain in his inflexible pride. He, too, cannot take people as they are, modify his stiff expectations. Unlike the captain, however, he is worked on by forces to which he must yield, the gentleness of Eleanora, the hardness of Lindkvist. He is humbled at last, and while we do not see him actually changed (for that would take another play; like Iago, he says not a word after his acknowledgment of defeat), we also do not see him go down finally. We can expect, however, since his will has not been so crumbled as Miss Julie's, since his degradation has been interior and private, that he will not take Miss Julie's ultimate solution to the enforced change of character, or collapse like the captain, all vitality spent.

Easter is a bridge between the realistic, sharp, clear-cut, monochromatic early plays (*The Father*, 1887; *Miss Julie*, 1888) and the surrealistic, complex, symphonic later plays (*A Dream Play*, 1902; *The Ghost Sonata*, 1907). The captain and Miss Julie offer portraits of persons unable, by any means, to yield to the requirements of reality. Elis does bend his nature. The large question then changes its character: just what is reality, to what are we yielding, just where and how do we live when we rise above our natures as we humble ourselves?

A *Dream Play* answers these questions in epical form. Whatever level we live on, whatever our occupations, "human life is pitiable." This melancholy refrain tolls throughout the play. Whatever we seek, whatever our ambitions, we are doomed to the repetition that "human life is to be pitied."

The daughter and the lawyer are depicted as married and living in an apartment adjoining his office. Their misery is unrelieved. An idiot girl, Kristin, goes around pasting up all cracks in the walls and windows to keep the heat of the apartment in. The baby's screaming frightens the clients. A cabbage smell permeates the apartment. The curtains, candlesticks, and chairs are awry. "It is not easy to be human," the wife says later after the lawyer describes how repetition turns "everything which was charming and witty and beautiful the night before" into the "ugly, stupid, repulsive. Pleasure stinks, and enjoyment falls to pieces. What people call success is always a step towards the next failure."

The secret behind the door, it is clear to us from the beginning, is that there is nothing behind the door. Theology, philosophy, medicine, law find nothing. Only the poet seems to understand this. The daughter tells him that "this world, its life and its inhabitants are . . . only a mirage, a reflection, a dream image." The poet asks the daughter, "before you go, tell me from what you suffered most down there." "From living," the daughter answers. "From feeling my vision dimmed by having eyes, my hearing dulled by having ears, and my thought, my airy, luminous thought, bound down in a labyrinth of fat. You have seen a brain. What twisting channels, what creeping ways!" And in her final summation, the daughter says:

> *This then it is to be a human being—*
> *ever to miss the thing one never prized*
> *and feel remorse for what one never did,*
> *to yearn to go, yet long to stay.*
> *And so the human heart is split in two,*
> *emotions by wild horses torn—*
> *conflict, discord, uncertainty.*

This would seem to be conclusively nihilistic. Out of himself, humbled into universality, the artist's only finding is that human life is to be pitied, that there is nothing behind the door of hope and expectation. But this itself is positive. To know that one is in a dream is not to expect the consequences and consolations of the real day. We cannot speak of a "logical" conclusion to *A Dream Play*. But the final resolution is one of a patient acceptance and resignation, a purging rather than a lingering discomfort. If this is the way life is, and we have neither to grant nor deny the possibility, then it is the way life is.

"The labor comes first," says the girl in *The Ghost Sonata*. "The labor of keeping the dirt of life at a distance." The dirt of life is everywhere, in deceit, in fruitless repetition, even in self-knowledge. "We are not what we seem," says the mummy, "because at bottom we are better than ourselves, since we detest our sins." We are doomed to the endless servitude of cleaning up after our vampirish servants, whether these serve us literally every day, or metaphorically, in the interest of our spirit and imagination. "Jesus Christ descended into hell," concludes the student. "That was His pilgrimage on earth."

The play is melancholy. We have unmaskings and deaths, tiredness and disillusion, frustration and disenchantment. Yet the student does not lose hope. "Where is anything that fulfills its promise? In my imagination." He feels the "vampire in the kitchen" beginning to suck him. Yet he can assert: "There are poisons that destroy the sight and poisons that open the eyes. I seem to have been born with the latter kind, for I cannot see what is ugly as beautiful, nor call evil good. I cannot." And when the girl is dying, he speaks to her in an accent of hope, of release, not resignation but expectation. "The Liberator is coming. Welcome, pale and gentle one. Sleep, you lovely, innocent, doomed creature, suffering for no fault of your own. Sleep without dreaming, and when you wake again . . . may you be greeted by a sun that does not burn, in a home without dust, by friends without stain, by a love without flaw."

But these are the ideals of earth itself, of life itself. It is the daily reward, and the agony of the play resides in the limitations of human possibility. Strindberg's plays move from the bitterness of personal anger to the hopelessness of the universal. This is a moral progression, and not simply because the universal is quantitatively more than the individual. The personal disaster, after all, matters not at all until it becomes a revelation of the total human disaster. Strindberg went from individuals and types to allegorical, all embracing, symbolic figures: an old man, a student, a mummy, a lawyer. The microscopically sharp question "Am I the father of my daughter?" is replaced by the questions without any particulars whatsoever: "What is behind the door? How escape the dirt of living?"

It is possible, conceivably, to answer the first sort of question; Ibsen and Shaw were constantly answering questions that were specific although the implications may have been larger. It is not possible, perhaps, to answer the second sort; but there is enough achievement and art in being able just to pose it. This Strindberg finally did.

3 CHEKHOV'S
MORALITY OF WORK

ONE LINE in *The Cherry Orchard* holds the play's essence. Lyubov is talking with Petya, the pedantic tutor of her drowned son. "My boy was drowned here," she says to him and weeps. "Pity me, my dear kind fellow." "You know I feel for you with all my heart," Petya replies stiffly. Her tears stopping, looking up, discontent, Lyubov chides him: "But that should have been said differently, so differently." Petya has spoiled the scene. Like an actor-director, Lyubov steps out of the action to criticize her partner. "But that should have been said differently, so differently." She is also troubled about his appearance. "You must do something with your beard to make it grow somehow," she laughs. "You look so funny." She is dramatically mercurial. She moves without pause from acting in tragedy to critical detachment.

The Cherry Orchard, in addition to whatever else it is, is ultimately a play exploring the tension between illusion and reality, between what seems and what is. The characters constantly see themselves in settings. They apostrophize things—a room, a chest, the cherry orchard itself—for these people have identity, like actors, only in a setting, in the three dimensional world of things. They are like Pirandello's six characters, fixed in a situation outside of which they have no independence. Their tragedy finally is that they are thrust into the world without their surrounding things, without their insulating stage setting (things themselves as well as the whole larger frame of feudal Russia itself) which defines them and sets them in motion. Lyubov's hope, apparently, is simply to construct another context for herself, in which as faithful mistress she will tend her sickly lover, in which the sweetly melancholy mother and daughter will read novels to each other while drinking tea. All characters not necessary for the new play need not report; they may go off any which way: Firs, the old retainer, to lie down, presumably just to die, right there on the stage, before the final curtain; Varya, the stepsister, to drift away, presumably to the nunnery she has mentioned. The expressed softness of heart of the main characters is just so much dramatic talk, part of the performance; it is not accompanied by the practical action required in the real world.

Lopahin is obviously from the real world, from the other side of the footlights, too obviously perhaps. He cannot understand the enchantment of the cherry orchard; he does not know what it means to have the estate written up in the "encyclopedia." It means nothing to him that Lyubov and Leonid and Anya have grown up here, have lived their lives surrounded by these walls and these things. He knows only that the orchard will come up for auction to satisfy unpaid bills. He is an outsider and as aware of this as the others are of being insiders. An outsider, his failing is that he does not know how to penetrate the setting. He would like to marry Varya; he is not unsuited to her, his practical sense is matched by hers. But he must have an intermediary to bring him through the curtain, and for a moment, Lyubov understands this, offers help, then flits away in her own drama, leaving both Lopahin and Varya alone, isolated. Both are, after all, minor personages for Lyubov; they will do to swell a scene for a moment, no more.

In small ways as well as in large, in minute details of background, and characterization, the text plays upon the tensions between romance and reality, between what seems, and what is, between the past (which is to say, memory), and the present, between what had been, and what is and will be. Charlotta Ivanovna right before our eyes performs feats of illusion, making Anya appear out of nowhere. But perhaps more marvelously she appears in her own person to tell us how insubstantial she is herself:

> I haven't a real passport of my own, and I don't know how old I am, and I always feel that I'm a young thing. When I was a little girl, my father and mother used to travel about to fairs and give solo performances — very good ones. And I used to dance *salto mortale,* and all sorts of things. And when papa and mamma died, a German lady took me and had me educated. And so I grew up and became a governess. But where I came from, and who I am, I don't know. . . . Who my parents were, very likely they weren't married. . . . I don't know (*takes a cucumber out of her pocket and eats*). I know nothing at all (*a pause*). One wants to talk, and has no one to talk to. . . . I have nobody.

Pulling cucumbers out of one's pockets may be a common enough Russian practice, but it seems here to emphasize with some piquancy the arbitrary, harlequinesque quality of her appearance and speech. And further to emphasize it, Epihodov, who speaks next, ignores her as if she were not there and had never spoken.

The drama of the brother and sister takes place between the poles represented by Lopahin, the concrete realist, and Trofimov, the abstract idealist. Neither Lopahin nor Trofimov is "wrong," but each represents an extreme. Both the practical and the ideal are necessary but in relation to other needs as well. The largest territory for living is between the poles. Trofimov is "above" the vulgar realities of beauty, and of love; he is pathetically silly in his pretensions; yet it is he who has as clear a sense of the future as the phlegmatic Lopahin. Lopahin for all his bourgeois grasping generously offers over and over again to help Lyubov and Gaev out of their difficulties, but he is simply never heard; actors do not hear the audience.

For a brief moment we think that the illusionists will be allowed to break out of their limitations, for Semyonov-Pishtchik, who also lives on expectations, a defining characteristic of romanticism, does indeed have his idle dreams come true. Expectations must always have some plausible basis. But Leonid and Lyubov themselves never gather more than a token sum from the faraway aunt, a minute fraction of the total necessary to redeem the estate. With the aunt's fifteen thousand roubles, they may surely be expected to begin another little drama, or perhaps to complete the one already hinted at, Lyubov's illicit liaison. The Ranevskys' expectations become all the more pathetically hollow as a result of Pishtchik's little triumph.

Chekhov in *The Cherry Orchard* is already feeling his way toward the Pirandellian theater, in which the very play itself, the whole convention of drama, is made part of the thematic statement. For a play is itself an artifice of romance, a contrived representation of reality, bearing a relationship to the actual in terms of possibilities and arrangements that may be controlled. *The Cherry Orchard*, then, while it is a play about the decay of the old feudal order, makes its point by depicting the fixed, inevitable, ineluctable futility of drama itself. Lyubov is trapped forever, doomed, on her stage; she cannot break out into the real world.

The characters in *The Cherry Orchard* move into, and out of their particular physical settings, however much they carry their own psychological world around with them. In *The Three Sisters*, the characters are frozen geographically as well as psychologically. We cannot so easily mistake the drama there as having simply to do with a transition in time, from feudalism to the modern world, or with a movement in space, from Paris to Russia and back. The three sisters never do get to Moscow, and, of course, we see that it does not matter at all. As Mary McCarthy put it, "The play is a study of the romantic character, and the city of Moscow is the earthly paradise, for which no railroad company can issue a ticket, no matter how prosperous the passenger may be." The conflict here, as it is made clear almost too explicitly throughout the play, is between what seems, illusion (Moscow), and what is, reality, the now and the here.

All appearances and desires are promptly contradicted in *The Three Sisters*. The physician knows no medicine. Olga longs for marriage while Masha, her sister, is wretched in hers. Irina longs for work, but it bores her when she gets it. Vershinin's wife keeps attempting suicide, the very repetition being a denial of the act.

Andrey is hopeful of a great name in learning, but the only accomplishment offered to us by his sisters is his making of a picture frame. The sisters do not follow through their expressed concern for their old servant when Natasha brutally berates her. Natasha is criticized early in the play for the vulgarity of her dress; just before the final curtain, she herself criticizes one of the three sisters for wearing a sash in bad taste.

Natasha is Lopahin with all sentiment removed.

She wears clashing combinations of colors because she does not look at herself in a mirror, in a setting. She does not see herself from the outside, as a spectator. She is firmly tending to her own hard business, scarcely aware that she is before any audience, scarcely aware of any drama. She is thus able, relentlessly, step by step, to take over the household in which everyone else is merely an actor.

Throughout the play, we hear the theme that things are not what they seem. "You say life is beautiful," ruminates Irina. "Yes, but what if it only seems so!" The doctor, in one of his drunken, muttered soliloquies says: "Perhaps it only seems to us that we exist, but really we are not here at all." The only characters in Chekhov who never have any doubts about their existence are those who never think, who live with their skins alone. For Chekhov, to think is almost not to be.

The Three Sisters has been accurately described as a study in futility, but it is such not simply because the sisters lose their possessions to Natasha, or because each has ambition squelched, but because nothing is what it appears to be, because each character's frustration, as in Hades, arises out of that character's deepest need. Having been trained to live in the realms of romance, the sisters find themselves in an all too real outpost of civilization. If they were indeed in Moscow, they might, for a time anyway, be caught up in the illusion of romance and importance and belonging which big cities bestow. But where they are, their foreign languages are useless, melting away, word by word, day by day, their special qualities of speech and bearing only airs.

Much has also been made of the fact that Chekhov was writing about a time of transition, the passing of the feudal and aristocratic old Russia to the communistic and proletarian new Russia. No doubt. We have in his plays people who are caught not only between the demands of romance and reality, but between the opposed demands of the old and the new. Chekhov's characters are defined by their longing, by their wishing for something beyond their reach, always separated from their goals by time or by space or by incapacities of character. Their inanition is the result of their too great self-consciousness. Like Pirandello's six characters—again—they are too acutely conscious of their particular kind of consciousness. But unlike Pirandello's six characters, who can still duplicate again and again the same moment of passion, Chekhov's people are somewhat more than figures; they are real enough to become bored by repetition, and they will break out of their paralysis if only for a moment. "For once in my life," murmurs Yelena as she embraces Astrov.

The Three Sisters, unlike *The Cherry Orchard*, which draws a picture only, offers an escape from fate: Work. The baron longs for work (although frustrated); Irina lusts for work, however bored she becomes, and we know that she will return to work; Olga moves steadily ahead by work. But the point about work is that one must not fool oneself about its meaning. It is a form of permanent therapy, meaningless in itself, perhaps as nihilistic as indolence itself, but a positive means of self-rescue from the wastelands of life, provided only that it is understood for what it is.

Uncle Vanya may be considered as studying the progress in Vanya from his false dependence on work before the play opens to his resigned but truer dependence on it at the end. *Uncle Vanya* is an essay examining the various possibilities of work and their implications as ways of finding meaning in a life which so often can seem a series of theatrical scenes only, clashes between what appears gloriously possible and what is ingloriously actual. Vanya happily devotes himself to his totally absorbing, backbreaking work on the estate in order to support the professor, who has the actor's self-confident capacity to overwhelm everyone with his importance. Vanya is not at all troubled by the work he has put in for so many years because it seems to him to have been in a noble cause, the support of the professor and his scholarship. But Vanya goes berserk when he realizes the true nature of the professor, his hollow pomposity, the emptiness of his achievement, and tries to shoot him. In the end, he returns to his work. In the last scene, the refrain of work, work, work, has a hysterical ring, for now it is softened by no illusion. It cuts and jabs and gashes with the harshness of the realization that it is in the cause of nothing. Work is its own end.

While Vanya at least for a period was driven by the illusion that his work has some important end, Yelena cannot fool herself.

SONYA Isn't there plenty to do? If only you cared to do it. . . . You could help us with the estate, teach the children or look after the sick. . . .

YELENA I don't know how to do such things. And they are not interesting. It's only in novels with a purpose that people teach and doctor the peasants. How am I, all of a sudden, à propos of nothing, to go and teach them or doctor them?

She may have been enchanted long enough to accept the old professor's proposal of marriage, but she is not fooled by others, nor certainly by herself. Her attitude toward her husband is one of plain, blunt, frank impatience, and we gather that she is tied to him not so much by a sense of form or of devotion, but by a very deep coldness of heart, by a monstrous indolence and indifference of character. Only once and only for a fleeting instant and only as a mere gesture does she allow feeling to flicker forth, and she snuffs it out at once. Her beauty obviously offers no ready remedy for the callous pointlessness of life, no more than Sonya's plainness and gentleness of heart.

Astrov denies the thesis that work is meaningful only in itself, but feebly. He delivers the longest speeches in the play, and these have to do with conservation, but not conservation merely as a hobby to occupy him, conservation as a means of relating to the future.

> But when I walk by the peasants' woods which I have saved from cutting down, or when I hear the rustling of the young copse planted by my own hands, I realize that the climate is to some extent in my power, and that if in a thousand years man is to be happy I too shall have had some small hand it it.

It seems to me especially meaningful that the most energetic, the most vital, the most balanced, the most intelligent, and, all in all, the most attractive person in the play carries the point that work as it has meaning after death is the only good and meaningful work that we can ultimately do. Yet the doctor is not himself altogether convinced of this. He calls himself a crank and concedes that his advocacy of conservation, the maps he draws, the statistics he gathers, are in the nature of a fanaticism. The map of Africa, vast and distant and unknown, throws a beam of triviality over the tableau. But the play has a more "positive" ending than *The Three Sisters*, which concludes with Olga's sigh, "If we only knew, if we only knew." Sonya apparently knows, for she speaks of rest coming only in death.

Are we to conclude, then, in the conventional way, that Chekhov is simply pessimistic? Certainly the characters in his plays incapable of self-awareness—

Lopahin, Natasha, the professor, the several kindly old servants—are not troubled by living. Introspection in itself seems a curse in Chekhov. But introspection happens also to be a way of discovery, of making contact with one's inner possibilities as these relate to the larger ones outside. If we are to find meaning in Astrov's strength as a person and character, perhaps we are to do this because Astrov reaches out, out, straining to engage with everyone, straining even to transcend time, to touch a future long after he is gone. Perhaps the only meaning in life is to be found in looking for meaning in life.

If Astrov is in any way an autobiographical possibility, then we might see a relation between Astrov's conservationism and Chekhov's playwriting, which both men practiced in addition to their medical work with peasants. To find meaning in mortal life, one must have an activity which has possibilities of immortality in more than a private way.

The Sea Gull is, of course, the most theatrical of all Chekhov's plays. If it had been written last, it might in parts even be taken as a parody of the Chekhovian manner. "Why do you always wear black?" asks Medvedenko of Masha, to open the play. "I am in mourning for my life," answers Masha. "I am unhappy." Since it is one of the early plays, it contains explicit material about the appearance-reality tension which we find implicitly embodied in the later ones. Chekhov moved from the issue of theatricality in the theater, as it affects artists, which is to say professionals working to make realities of illusions, to the issue of theatricality, or romanticism, or exaggerated self-consciousness, as it affects the somewhat larger population of nonprofessionals engaged in somewhat the same sort of enterprise, that of making illusion viable. For as it did to Pirandello, the question of the theater

—of how much is real, of how much is illusion, of the intermingling of the two, of their symbiotic dependence, of their confusions—became for Chekhov the question of life itself. He submerged the specifically theatrical aspects of the question he knew as an artist beneath the more universal ones belonging to the larger society he knew as a physician and as a man.

We can scarcely miss the theatrical emphasis of *The Sea Gull*. A stage occupies the stage and on it we see the beginning of a play, and through its arches we see the landscape beyond. (This is precisely the stage within the stage device of Pirandello's *Each in His Own Way*.) Madame Arkadina, the great actress, when it appears she may be losing Trigorin, turns on her theatrical magic to enchant her lover—and, simultaneously, to demonstrate to us her powers as an actress (in one of the rare occasions in literature in which a person asserted to be great actually proves himself to be so). Characters over and over again announce that they are moving in nightmares, in dreams. And here as later, persons pretend to be something other than they are. Madame Arkadina, for example, insists that she is a pauper when in fact she is well-to-do, pretending to be only a few years older than her own son. As in Pirandello, some of the most significant lines seem to be spoken directly to the audience: the end of Act II, in which Nina "advances to the footlights" and says "It's a dream!"; and the conclusion of the play itself, in which the suicide of Madame Arkadina's son is announced over the footlights, away from the principals.

But these are all details setting the context for the two tragedies: the suicide of Treplev, the collapse of Nina. For both are the victims of the destructive impulses implicit in the creative force. At the end of Act II, after the hero-worshipping Nina has paid her awestruck homage to Trigorin, the famous playwright, Trigorin makes a note for a story. "A subject for a short story," he tells Nina: "a young girl, such as you, has lived all her life beside a lake; she loves the lake like a sea gull, and is as free and happy as a sea gull. But a man comes by chance, sees her, and having nothing better to do, destroys her like that sea gull there." Nina's fate seems to be determined as much by her excessive worship of the theater and art as by Trigorin's making of his contact with her the beginning of a literary piece which records her actual end. "A man came by chance," she babbles in Act IV, "saw a [sea gull] and, just to pass the time, destroyed it. . . . A subject for a short story. . . ." She is given a role to work out in life itself, and she takes it.

Trigorin, of course, can no more recall his shooting of the sea gull and his having it stuffed than he can fully recall the quality of his contact with Nina. His involvement with her was tangential, its shallowness and brevity determined by his art. Its beginnings were necessary, to be sure, for all the reasons he gives. Her vitality, her enthusiasm, her youthful loveliness transport him into the dream of art. Its end was equally necessary, for novelty is novelty only just so long, and it was only the freshness and newness, the passing nature of the relation, which brought it into being in the first place. Callousness? Not really, since Trigorin spends so very much time making explicit to Nina the peculiarly, hideously compulsive character of his work.

But nevertheless it is the neglect of Nina's existence as a person who is more than merely a young girl ambitious for artistic fame that causes her ruin. Neither Nina nor the others, with the one exception of Treplev (himself unfulfilled), take Nina for what she is. Cast out by her parents, forgotten by her lover, she is doomed.

Treplev's fate is similar. He is the son of the incredibly magnetic, incredibly vain, magnificently talented actress, Madame Arkadina. Madame Arkadina lives completely only in the theater. "It's nice being with you, my friends, charming to listen to you," she can audaciously say to her host and her friends, "but . . . to sit in a hotel room somewhere and learn one's part is ever so much better." Madame Arkadina scarcely has the wish to recognize in any appropriate way her grown son. His age denies her youth, his hints of obscure talent distress her. She would much rather he remained an artist manqué, hidden on her brother's estate. And after he has begun to achieve some small fame, she can casually declare *while idling her time away with lotto:* "Only fancy, I have not read anything of his yet. I never have time."

And, of course, Treplev is caught up in that daisy chain of futility so common in Chekhov. It is his fate to love Nina, who does not love him but loves Trigorin, who does not love her but loves Madame Arkadina. Treplev himself is loved by Masha whom he cannot love in return; Masha is loved by her husband, Medvedenko, whom, of course, she holds in cruel contempt. And to intensify this round of frustration, her mother loves Dorn, who, anticlimactically, loves no one.

Chekhov's short stories do not achieve the epical sweep of his plays because they lack the theatrical texture. The absurdity of modern man's place in the world may possibly best be described in the idiom of the theater. Compare the harrowingly blank moral nature of Ivanov with the shallow emptiness of some of Katherine Mansfield's heartless heroes (*e.g.,* "The Man Who Had No Heart"). Precisely because the essence of the theater has traditionally been in conflict of some sort, the aimlessness, the futility, the impotence of Chekhov's people become agonizing. For all the action—the shootings, and suicides, and duels, and fires, and general nastiness—there is no action. Nothing brings about changes. The characters do not change, do not reach out of their fate to entangle themselves with another's fate. For all their graciousness of manner, they are selfishly piratical of soul. Those that have the capacity to act generously, to offer solace and charity, are paralyzed or blinded in their dim, constricted world of self.

Uncle Vanya connects the theme of the theatricality of life with its consequent disaster and the theme of salvation in meaningful work for the future. The first item on any philosopher's agenda must be to define the problem. In his exploration of theatrical confusion as the source of futility and final tragedy in modern life, Chekhov seems to have defined the problem in at least one way. His offered solution would seem to be valid also if we take his enterprise as a playwright as his own contribution of meaningful work for the future.

4 SHAW'S
MORAL SERIOUSNESS

SHAW, early in his career as dramatist, insisted that he was not an artist but a teacher. What he meant, of course, was that he did not write simply to please; he declared that he was not a "beauty monger"; he wanted to teach. But his teaching was rarely just polemical, offering only some particular dogma or revelation; he could never be anything so simple as a salesman for evolution, or for "the new woman," or for socialism, causes which, at one time or another, together with others, he did espouse and attempt to interpret. His teaching, like all good teaching perhaps, reduced itself to the message that only the hardest truth, the barest reality, can "make us free," only truth can make us fulfill our promise as man.

This insistence on truth becomes finally nothing less than a moral passion in Shaw, a passion devoted to changing the man's sense of self. For Shaw, the fulfilled, the nearly complete man is the one whose vision and apprehension have not been blurred by expectations, by poverty, by private and social insecurities, by uncertainties of identity, by limitations of intelligence or instinct. Shaw's "truth" was never abstract, the scientist's or the artist's detached perfection; it was a truth whose validity lay in the service of man, in the furtherance of all those axiomatic human values we cannot even name any longer without risking the charge of sentimentality.

What made Caesar great, Shaw insisted in *Caesar and Cleopatra*, was his "originality," his capacity to see things more "truly" than other men. But while Caesar himself keeps making this point endlessly throughout the play, in quips and epigrams and little speeches (Caesar is stuffy about his capacity for originality), his most moving speech in the play, an outburst emotional with bitterness, has to do with man's inhumanity to man (it comes just after Cleopatra has had Pothinus murdered in a casual gesture of vengefulness). Truth for Shaw, as for Caesar, must have an end, and this end can be nothing less than enabling man to see himself whole and in a larger perspective than that of the particular moment and its narrow needs.

Partial, particularized visions, however compelling, were abhorrent to Shaw. The Catholic spokesmen in *Saint Joan* (except for the obviously demented and stupid ones) have reason and rhetoric all on their side in their opposition to Joan. Like Joan, we cannot easily resist the force of their logic and indeed of their quite genuine concern for Joan. Yet it is with Joan that we finally sympathize, for she is more than mere idea; she is so much more than the savior of France, the unconscious opponent of feudalism, the threat to the Church; she, like so many of Shaw's other leading men and leading ladies, is a heroine of life itself. The "salvation" offered her by the court is the surrender of daily, spontaneous, full living; for Joan imprisonment is no less a destruction than death itself; in fact, it is a worse destruction, a lingering one, an "unnatural" one.

The greatest threat to man's achievement of truth, as Shaw saw it, was society, and it was natural that he should have written most of his plays to examine various aspects of the conflict between the individual and society. Yet he was careful never to be limited by "theme," by the rationale of a special circumstance. Insisting that he wrote specifically for his own time and his own place, he always transcended the momentary and the local.

Major Barbara, for example, comes closest of any of Shaw's plays that can be readily produced to being allegorical. The munitions village is out of Wells or Huxley. We are to contrast the cleanness, modernity, healthfulness, "enlightenment" of the factory with the dirtiness, superstition, and squalor of the Salvation Army. Shaw is pushing the paradox almost to the breaking point, and complicating it considerably, by contrasting the two kinds of salvation, the one offered by the army of religion, the other by the makers of ammunition.

Undershaft is not quite in the same business as Mrs. Warren; his profession is both worse and better. Undershaft is a moralist and philosopher; Mrs. Warren is a practical business woman. She is sharp, unsentimental, aware of the world. She does not justify her profession except in "average" practical terms. She does not play games, as Undershaft does, in his offer of the huge gift to the Salvation Army, in his "gambling" with his daughter for Bill Walker's soul. The simple—and eternal—question posed by both Mrs. Warren's cartel and by Undershaft's is whether good can ever come from bad. I don't think Shaw ever resolves this question, which is abstract anyway, here or elsewhere. But the question is transformed to relate to realities which are too concrete, too oppressive, to dismiss in favor of high-floating ideas.

Undershaft (like Mrs. Warren) shifts the discussion away from the evil involved in munitions making (prostitution) to that implicit in poverty. The major crime against humanity, both finally insist, is poverty, for poverty destroys the human possibility, and does so invisibly, as it were, with the indifference and connivance of society. To say this is by no means to forgive warmongering or organized prostitution; in fact, these extreme methods to fight poverty all the more condemn it. You can fight poverty, you can fight the mangling of the soul, *even* with a munitions factory, even with a chain of bordellos.

Yet Shaw is so very much the writer about social issues, of the individual's relations to sweeping problems of society, it is natural to neglect, even to overlook, his essential concern with the moral relations among individuals, relations which ultimately may have little directly to do with society but provide it with its entire moral tone.

The plot of *Pygmalion* when separated from the theme depends, after all, on the peculiar intimacy that develops between a man congenitally unable to lose himself in love and a woman quite normal and responsive. Shaw was contrasting Pygmalion's involvement with Galatea, which was not so detached and objective as an artist's relation with his product should be, with Higgins's cooler, more purely esthetic relation with Liza Doolittle. The truest, most totally classical artist is not carried away by his work. Moreover—to bring in the most obvious theme of *Pygmalion*, that social differences are merely superficial, that a flower girl can be mistaken for a duchess when outfitted with appropriate speech, manners, and clothes—it would certainly be self-defeating for Higgins to be taken in by his own hoax, so to speak. He does know Liza's origins. He knows better than anyone else that there must certainly be a difference between surface and depth, that Liza, while she may never be as false as

Freddie's sister, also could never be as genuine as his own mother.

But having said all this, having stated dramaturgic and logical explanations for the lack of fulfillment in the Higgins-Liza pairing (and remembering Shaw's own sequel in which he pairs Liza off with Freddie), we still have to account for the peculiar poignancy that we sense in the relationship, Liza's refusal to accommodate to Higgins's coldness, Higgins's incapacity to feel emotionally toward Liza. The confrontation scenes between the two at the end of the play are most moving in their depiction of two attractive persons in every way apparently suited for each other, unable for the most unyielding reasons to break the bonds of their separate paralyses. And there is here, too, the additional irony in showing Higgins as devoid of the expected passion; it is he who is finally less than human; it is he who would need the intercession of a deity to be turned from marble to man. This study of the relationship of two highly particularized human beings underlies and gives importance to the more obvious elements of the play.

We can indeed be so misled by obvious elements in Shaw as sometimes scarcely to be aware of fundamental matters. Consider *The Doctor's Dilemma.* Just what is that dilemma? Certainly it is easy enough to put it in the terms most immediately clear: shall the doctor save the worthy but mediocre man Blenkinsop, or the worthless but very talented one, Dubedat? But the play is surely about more than this somewhat sophomoric opposition, which is even at one point put in an example that might arise at a dormitory bull session. In spite of all its farce and jocularity, the play is about the irresponsibility of physicians. The doctors not only impose their professional crotchets on their patients—stimulate the phagocytes, remove the nuciform sac—but they impose also their personal lusts. Sir Colenso's choice—*the* doctor's dilemma—between Blenkinsop and Dubedat with ultimate and bitter irony has nothing whatsoever to do with the question of whose life is worth more for civilization.

Sir Colenso's dilemma, which is his alone, an entirely private one, is put quite casually and thus with incredible heartlessness, and has to do with his being in love with Dubedat's wife. He does not have the good taste to put it, even for Sir Patrick, on a higher plane. He is ready to kill Dubedat—quite honorably, it is true, if diabolically, by putting him in the hands of a fellow practitioner who is notoriously incompetent— for no such moral principle as that a good man, however much a whining, self-pitying, sopping rag he might be, is more worth saving than a bad one, no matter how great a genius he might be. Nothing of the sort. Sir Colenso merely wants to marry Jennifer Dubedat and is quite sure that she will have him too.

His monumental conceit, his villainy, are sharply underscored at the conclusion, in the epiloguelike last act, when he discovers that Mrs. Dubedat has married someone else. It is Sir Colenso's incredible, solipsistic conceit that we catch in this final scene when we learn the futility of his decision. The fact that even he might not have saved Dubedat's life, given Shaw's premise that all medicine is quackery and that particular cures are fads, merely makes the villainy that much blacker. Sir Colenso genuinely believed he could save Dubedat. The moral filthiness of Sir Colenso raises the play to the level of grotesque, macabre comedy, a tone much more in harmony with the cranky, bilious, often petty introduction. The bland yet sinister presence of Sir Colenso nearly eclipses any "social" issue in modern medicine.

Goodness in Shaw, like badness, is more a personal

and individual matter than a social one. What are we to make of *Androcles and the Lion*, which is a delightful, childlike, romping farce about, of all things, Christians marching to their martyrdom? Yet it is not shallow, let alone blasphemous, at all, and it is, indeed finally very serious, in spite of the picture of an emperor being chased by a lion and of a tailor waltzing with one. I would argue that the play's very frivolity, its slapstick, is essential to its seriousness, for what Shaw here demonstrates is the common humanness of all mankind, past and present, great and small, of whatever creed. Lavinia's eloquent but emotional description of the nature of her Christian faith—just as she cannot clasp a mouse, so she cannot bring her arm to drop a pinch of incense on a pagan altar—is effective because we can understand this instinctive response very well, as apparently the Roman captain does too, where we might not be able to understand so well a more compelling but more lofty and more reasoned theological argument. (Compare here Dick Dudgeon's instinctive incapacity to betray the Reverend Anderson even though he knows this is illogical and suicidal.) *Androcles* is a child's play, and it comes to us through our vestigial child's sympathy. In his goodness, submissiveness, gentleness, Androcles is a child's hero, and the way he conquers power and brutality through love is the world's best way.

One need hardly say that Shaw is a playwright of ideas, but the ideas gain their force precisely because they are embodied in the emotional and immediate. Consider *Man and Superman*. The play, except for the occasional outbursts about the Life Force and the references to one or another current issue, is really a straight enough Edwardian farce, legitimately classifiable in the company of Oscar Wilde's work. The scene in hell is rambling, discursive even for Shaw, highly abstract, and as high in genuine philosophic tone as the play is low in it. Are we to take the interlude as an appendage similar to a Shavian preface or sequel, stimulating but irrelevant, perhaps even to be dismissed as having no artistic justification? I think not. It is Don Juan, Jack Tanner's other incarnation, who carries the burden of the meaning of the hell scene.

We are asked to see Don Juan in his traditional image, a figure outside moral society, to be equated, one supposes, with such Shavian creations as Louis Dubedat, Dick Dudgeon, Caesar, Marchbanks, and Jack Tanner himself. All of the latter figures, however, are still mortal, on the way perhaps to the enlightenment of Don Juan, but in their various ways not nearly so complete, so perfect, as Don Juan. Only the man filled to brimming with realizing the mortal possibilities can know both the importance and unimportance of them. A Don Juan rejecting pleasure makes a more compelling case than an ascetic doing so. John Tanner has a long way to go to be Don Juan, for he is plainly identified as a man who is always putting words and ideas between himself and experience, sometimes indeed, as in the scene involving Violet's honor, simply baffled by the variety of possibilities in reality. For all that, it is Tanner who, Shaw indicates, will find his way to the height of Don Juan, for he does think, he does articulate, and presumably he can feel, he can be carried away by passion of a sort, as is plain from the scene in which Ann Whitefield finally pries him out of his thick shell of words. It is the thinking, feeling human being, then, who holds the future of the race, who can realize, as Don Juan says, that after all the pleasures are done with, when, indeed, it becomes pointless to pursue pleasures, as in heaven, it is man's highest task which asserts itself, the need to use one's mind fully.

The devil and Don Juan do not disagree about man's worldly situation. Their opposition is to be found in the meaning of man's pettiness, foolishness, wickedness. The devil is sentimentally resigned about the possibility in man for improvement. He offers nothing but escape from horror. Don Juan relentlessly insists that the horror must be confronted and overcome, that overcoming evil in the world is a divine imperative. Man has a mind as well as a body and, while it may be difficult for mind to control or even understand body, it is the only way to salvation.

Shaw's heaven and hell, like the gulf between them, are parables for earthly states. Hell *is* a city much like Seville. Hell is also the mortal state of mind in which there are easy, loose, casual, self-indulgent pleasures, ideas, responses, with which one can smugly relax, lulled into a dangerous security, lulled into misconceiving such a state as heaven. "Heaven" is a hard place, offering no ready arrangements of things, insisting on an endless examination and reexamination of them, demanding an unflinching, unblinking viewing of truth, promising nothing but the reward of the effort itself, *yet all the time acknowledging the ultimate importance, the divinity, of man.*

Now, Don Juan's philosophy must be understood against the background of the play, with all its very human foolishness and brightness: life comes first and must come fully, but it must be succeeded by the thought, understanding, interpretation that comes after experience and with remoteness; on the other hand, the play must be understood as not final by any means in its handling of experience, for events, with thought, analysis, and time, will move toward the possibility of a Don Juan, who knows better than his partners in hell when to give up mortal urgings and accept the responsibility of immortality. Stripped of its topical allusions to evolution, the emancipation of women, the rise of the working class, etc., etc., *Man and Superman* seems to me Shaw's most triumphant assertion of the moral import of truth.

Candida is perhaps Shaw's most masterful blending of ideas with persons. The play may be most revealingly approached through the varying attitudes toward reality of the principal characters. In the early moments of the play, we have the confrontation of Morell and Burgess. Morell's "idealism," if one may even begin to use such a word for the softness of his values, is corrupt to the point of sentimentalism; Burgess's "realism" is corrupt to the point of cynicism. We can no more believe in Morell's cloying sense of his fairy-tale marriage than we can in Burgess's depraved notions about commerce among human beings. Sentimentalism with its rose-colored glasses and cynicism with its black ones are extremes of response to reality, and as such essentially neat and simple. Sentimentality and cynicism, Morell and Burgess, make up the devil of *Man and Superman*. Morell and Burgess define the boundaries, then, of the possibilities in relating to the world. If Morell has never left his satin-lined crib, Burgess has never allowed himself to emerge from the gutter.

There is an early confrontation, too, between Marchbanks and Candida in terms of their responses to reality, although the issues here are more subtle and more shaded. Marchbanks's realism is poetic; he refuses to compromise with anything mundane, much less with anything sordid or shabby or in any way less than perfect. Candida asks for a mother-of-pearl inlaid scrubbing brush; he offers instead a boat to realms of beauty. (His "poetry," it should be noted, is anything but the sentimental lyricism of Morell. It is hard and real and clearly respected by Shaw.) Marchbanks's poetic realism, incapable of traffic with prose in any form, is opposed to the accommodating realism of Candida. Candida adapts to everything; she absorbs all. She accepts not only ugly onions and scrubbing brushes but Marchbanks's poetry and Morell's socialism; and she accepts these things within her capacity, which is to say altogether nonintellectually, making the acceptance all the more complete since where there is no understanding, there can be no doubt.

Candida is exceptional as a play of ideas in that the ideas are so totally immersed in the characters. In *Candida*, conflict is personal, that is, dramatic; the opposition of the varying ideas is hardly intellectual, not even between Marchbanks and Morell, who flare up at each other physically at one moment. We do not have here the open debate of the scene in hell. But throughout, the characters are the persons they are because of their ideas. Marchbanks, pulsatingly responsive to beauty, describes himself—with typically Shavian, unself-conscious accuracy—as a "nervous disease"; in his sensitivity he is as raw as a wound. Morell is cloaked in layers of armor, which shield him from reality, which filter his contact with it. His rhetoric serves as a sentimentally distorting screen between himself and it. Burgess—a caricature of the new bourgeois—is grotesque in his vulgar shrewdness; he is most nearly idea and man in one: the most functional and calculating in his relations with people, he understands not at all those not in the same sphere as his and so serves as a baffled but self-possessed comic commentator, speaking "asides," to whom everyone else seems reasonably "mad." Candida, of course, represents the archetypal woman, the eternal feminine in her capacious domesticity. Shaw romantically disburdens her of her two children, who never appear. Onstage, she mothers only grown men.

The manner of the play, of course, is comic, yet the ending is possibly tragic, and in this opposition may be found its moral intention. There is a strict order of value in the attitudes toward reality of the four principal characters. With Morell you get an attitude that one might almost call evil if it were not so flabby. He is a huge baby in his adaptation to the world. Burgess, no baby, no soft sentimentalist, is a man completely without idealism, without any sense of an idea, without hope, or the notion of hope, without any confidence in human goodness or the possibility of it. There is a kind of animal adaptability about him; he is constantly changing color with his background. But his own original background accompanies him everywhere. His cynicism is necessary to his talent, but it also distorts his vision. He may provoke in us the same good-humored response at any moment—as Undershaft does, as Mr. Doolittle does, as the devil does in *Man and Superman*—but it is a provocation that comes from a diabolical view of things.

If Shaw does not condemn Candida's view of things, he does not either altogether approve of it. Like her father, her response also is an animal one to things, in her case protective and domestic rather than suspicious and destructive, but instinctual nevertheless. "Natural," Shaw calls her.

Marchbanks's is the highest level of response to reality. Although he is complex, he is young, eighteen years old. He starts with the most highly developed, most acute, most honest response to things, but he starts in late adolescence. Part of his superior view of reality is that he can change, and does; the others are fixed in their responses. At the beginning of the second act, Marchbanks is presented almost in a soliloquy; he all but steps forth and addresses the audience. The subject of his address is the need for loving and being loved. It is always troublesome to respond to such discussions in Shaw, for he clearly means them to be taken seriously. Shaw is perhaps no less a believer in the power of love, in love being at the roots of true morality, than is D. H. Lawrence. (The combat between Jack Tanner and Ann Whitefield, in *Man and Superman*, is perhaps as sexually intense as anything in Lawrence, although the rhetoric in which it is conducted is totally different. And Marchbanks's intimacy with Candida is based on their ability to communicate below—and above—the level of conversation.) Marchbanks wants continuing love and continuing relations between people. This is what he wants from Candida and can give her. For him nothing else signifies. Marchbanks cannot yet understand what Shaw and Candida understand, that we cannot reject everyday things just because they are not right or not beautiful. In this Marchbanks shows no failing of character, but only his immaturity and inexperience. We know that Marchbanks will easily learn what mere age can teach. He will not turn out to be like Burgess, cynical, distrustful, negative.

Marchbanks wants a reciprocal continuing love from Candida; he wants this without adulteration and rejects as evil anything which lessens or inhibits it. Perhaps this is an imperfect view of reality, but it is not an ignoble one. It is the only one that does not have to compromise with what may be merely momentary and "practical" need. Marchbanks matures in the course of the play in that he realizes at the end that not only can he do without Candida, who embraces Morell, but that he must do without her. Candida, every bit as magnificent as Marchbanks has thought her to be, must remain true to her character, which is to mother Morell, and cannot put aside this need of hers in order to accept what Marchbanks has to offer. Perhaps he is contemptuous in speaking to her of his "secret"; but he seems to have matured sufficiently to be *merely* understanding of her (which, coming after passion, is little more than contempt anyway). The essential paradox here is that the eighteen-year-old fragile, effeminate poet is the man in the play, and we are forced to see that he is the only free person in it.

Candida's assertion of responsibility, her denial of any self-satisfying impulse to accede to the poet's proposition, is to be contrasted, it seems to me, with Nora's leaving her family in *The Doll's House*. Nora breaks up a family for the sake of an idea, a very compelling one no doubt, but her largely intellectual act possibly throws doubt on the strength of her instincts before it. Candida, never intoxicated by principles, responds exactly as we should expect after observing her continual disregard of intellect throughout the play. (Of course, I am distinguishing "intellect," the articulation of responses and issues, from "intelligence." Candida's intelligence is prodigious.) Both Morell and Marchbanks are big babies, ready to break up a household—with all the concomitant ruin—to carry out the logic of their principles. But Candida cannot be simple-minded with such serious stakes. She will, for a moment, seem to allow herself to fall in with the dramatic choice being staged by Marchbanks and Morell. An accommodating woman, she works it out in terms of the immediate alternatives offered her. We know very well that she would never leave her husband—*were he ten times genuinely stronger than the poet*. Marchbanks senses this. His secret may be just this, that he alone finally understands Candida.

Marchbanks, stoic poet that he is, is defeated; Candida chooses not to follow what may, after all, be her deepest and most genuine instinct; the shallow Morell is smugly triumphant in defeat. Morell's victory alone is enough to sound the tragic note. Candida's brief attempt to force Morell into some degree of masculine assertion is as heroic as his density makes her failure tragic.

Shaw himself created the problem of our recognizing his seriousness, for to work most effectively he had, as it were, to appear not to be working. He insisted on being taken as "journalist," to use his own word, scoffing at estimates of his genius which concentrated on his literary artistry, and used his enormous skill to embody inherently distasteful matter in appealing form. One result was, as has been said, that his public licked off the sugar coating and spit out the pill, and, of course, very often it did not even know that there was a pill. But Shaw couldn't have cared less about being considered clown or prophet, for his concern was with his effect and not with his appearance.

Without ever becoming lost or involved in abstract, esthetic experiment, or any art for art's sake movement, he was one of the world's great artists. He always directed his genius—in his plays, in his music and in his dramatic criticism, in his assorted later writings—to one of the great objects of any art, moral affirmation.

The plays, more vitally than any of his writings which explicitly devoted themselves to social and moral questions, illustrate the character and range of his moral seriousness, for they depict men and women in situations of life and of social history. Like Ibsen and Chekhov, Shaw was always concerned with the individual's response in a social situation; but less obviously, he was like Henry James as well in his awareness of an individual's responsibility to himself and to other individuals. Yet he differed from Ibsen, Chekhov, and James fundamentally, for he never lost or seriously modulated his hopefulness in mankind and his awareness of its potential for goodness. He intertwined the various aspects of social and individual morality in everything he wrote: morality for him was not divisible; the social and personal were ultimately one. And finally and most importantly, he always implicitly offered a way to achieving moral understanding in his unrelenting emphasis on an honesty related to essential reality.

Like all of Shaw's genuinely moral heroes, Caesar is an amoral man, but amoral only in terms of practiced and accepted morality. Like Tanner and Undershaft, Caesar appears above the world's rules in order to prove himself not indifferent to their intent and to the motives which originally prompted them. "Having virtue," Shaw says of his Caesar, "he had no need of goodness," meaning by goodness the cheapjack morality of unoriginal men. Could one ever take the Reverend Morell, for example, as seriously as one takes Caesar at the moment of his outburst at Cleopatra? Morell's morality, which, of course, can be nothing but impressively sincere, is trivial by comparison with Caesar's. The former is inimical to any true morality, the latter indispensable.

It may be argued that Shaw's moral involvement is limited by his emphasis on logic, by his preeminent and crystalline common sense, by his apparent negation of emotion. "Shaw's passion," writes the editor of a volume of Shaw's prose, "was of the head, not the heart." And indeed a creation like Higgins—and even like Tanner—seems to support such a conclusion. Yet Higgins is clearly depicted as an incomplete, an unfulfilled man. He represents the epitome of a cold logic which can never get itself so heated by simple, common values as to invent an easy pattern for living.

But the fact that Higgins is not positively evil does not absolve him from Shaw's dismissal of him as a human being. "Galatea never does quite like Pygmalion," Shaw concludes his epilogue to the play; "his relation to her is too godlike as to be altogether agreeable." Eliza is human; Higgins, not.

Tanner, who is a more complex and richer personality than Higgins, cannot divest himself of natural passion, for all his talk. The Life Force sweeps him up. Shaw never made much of physical attraction between men and women, but he paid it the highest regard by accepting it as so fundamentally given as not to require emphasis. Sex for Shaw in *Pygmalion, Man and Superman, The Doctor's Dilemma, Misalliance,* any number of other plays, is the assumed breeding place for the entanglements his characters have to straighten out. And very often sex provides moral perspective to a whole assortment of themes, as in *Man and Superman,* say, or *The Doctor's Dilemma.* Shaw always used his head to further the projects of his heart, and he tried never to let his heart turn his head. He would simply not pair off Eliza and Higgins, for, as he explains, that might well have been disastrous for both—aside from being implausible except on the most obvious penny romance level.

It is a work of labor and, occasionally, some daring to apprehend the full measure of seriousness in Shaw. Such an apprehension requires working with the material and nature of his art on a far subtler, more complex, more committed basis perhaps than that required even by artists like Joyce and Eliot. Shaw always proves disturbing, for in spite of his Jovian optimism, he puts the burden of felicity and salvation ultimately on the reader. The moment of crisis in Shaw occurs outside the work as well as within it. The reader cannot remain passive and still respond to

Shaw's art. He must work out the moral point and understand it—and be prepared to run the risk of absorbing it—for himself. In this respect, Shaw demands no less of us than any prophet.

THE MODERN TRAGICOMEDY
   OF WILDE AND O'CASEY

THE PLAYS of Oscar Wilde tempt facile formulation.
Louis Kronenberger, for example, in his survey of English comedy, speaks of *Lady Windermere's Fan* as
"fashionable trash." Even Shaw, who seemed uneasily
aware that there was more to Wilde than met the
common eye, called him "heartless." Mary McCarthy,
who came close to suggesting that Wilde was touching on some of the themes of existential drama,
echoed Shaw's charge of heartlessness and concentrated on Wilde's manner. Wilde's manner does blind
one, but as in any valid art, manner is ultimately
matter. A view of Wilde in the company of O'Casey
suggests an obscured moral dimension in Wilde; it
may also help us see aspects of O'Casey in bolder
perspective.

   Wilde's matter is obviously concerned with the individual in a particular society, of course, a society
obsessed by status, identity, limits of behavior. *The
Importance of Being Earnest* is, among other things,
an account of the search of several young persons for
meaning in a society extraordinarily reluctant, even
impotent, to assign importance to anything except the
superficial. The dominant atmosphere, as in Sartre's
No Exit, as in the settings of Beckett, is boredom,
emptiness, a despair of experiencing genuine feeling.

And because the characters rarely know what to do with themselves, other than indulge their impulses, the compulsion to wisecrack becomes pathological, onanistic, a substitute for feeling, thought, and behavior. The very cleverness becomes the action of the play, as when the principals pause in the repartee to comment on it.

The motivating force of the action is the absurd. The two young ladies insist on falling in love with and marrying young men who bear the name of Ernest; no other name will do. With "other babies," to quote one of them, the young men are ready to go off to be rechristened. Jack Worthing, when an infant, was exchanged for a three-volume novel. And if this is not enough to indicate to us the "literary" source of the action, we have the two young ladies arranging the events of their world in the diaries they keep. In short, the characters, while serving within the heart of conventional society, determine their own identity and fate, whenever possible, on the basis of self-indulgent whim, but a whim strictly confined within the value limits of that society. This is the sort of absurd hell Shaw described in *Man and Superman*, an "infernal Arcadia," as Mary McCarthy called it, a domain where the merest and shallowest longing is at once lavishly gratified.

Naturally, then, all things in the Wildean world have to be glorious, richly damasked, royally colored, elegantly arranged, sumptuously detailed, everywhere candied. Cecil Beaton's luxurious design for the Broadway production of *Lady Windermere's Fan* was a triumph of communication; it said almost as much as the play itself. The setting was applauded before a character appeared. The film of *The Importance of Being Earnest* was an elaborate exercise in the delights of color, of cultivated lawns and trees, extravagant costumes, beautiful young people. And always, obviously, there is the dazzle in Wilde of the sheer text, of words and phrases meticulously arranged to shine and flash. Wilde's text has been perceptively called verbal opera, and we do regularly hear the melody of sheer language. Lady Bracknell not only rings the bell with a Wagnerian authority; her speeches sound like the arias of a Wagnerian contralto (or maybe tenor).

But Wilde is better than Maugham or Coward or Pinero or Jones or Kaufman, all of whom could write bright dialogue or construct intricate plots, because there lurks in the Wildean text a consciousness of the hellishness of all the activity and talk. In *The Importance of Being Earnest*, the two young men expect to find no pleasures in conventional society; they must go "Bunburying"; that is, they must leave their world and seek elsewhere for private satisfactions, which are never specified. They are required by the social trap to go through various motions, including courtship, and they sacrifice their private needs, wiping out their independent identity, willingly immolating themselves, causing themselves to assume new names, new identities. They move into the heart of a society which they despise, which they have for years been escaping, which they help depict for us as tawdry, dishonest, tyrannical, stupid, superficial.

And it is because of the horror which we sense in this society that *Lady Windermere's Fan* may be read as a peculiarly modern tragedy, or near-tragedy, which rises above the "melodrama" Kronenberger describes it as being. It is melodrama only if we allow ourselves to accept the same estimate of that society which determines Mrs. Erlynne, Lord Windermere, and Lady Windermere, after all the evidence persuading us not to accept it. The attempts of the brilliant and beautiful Mrs. Erlynne to get back into the society which banished her are shabby and pathetic. She seems to have learned so little about the values of that society that her appeal to her daughter not to leave her husband and child is based principally on the punishment attendant on ostracism from it. The "worldly" Mrs. Erlynne never once tries to find out whether Lady Windermere might indeed love Lord Darlington; she never once tries to elicit from her daughter the nature of her true feelings for her husband or for her "lover." For all her worldliness, she remains enslaved by provincial standards of feeling and conduct. Her home province, of course, is that small area of Edwardian society which appears in Shaw mainly for purposes of burlesque, in *Major Barbara* and *Pygmalion*.

Mrs. Erlynne's character and past are ambiguous. She may well be guilty of that hypocrisy Wilde speaks of, in having a wicked reputation while never doing anything bad. If her earlier transgression had been no more than Lady Windermere's, merely showing up in a gentleman's apartment out of pique at suspecting her husband of infidelity, as we are given to understand, then she is scarcely the fallen woman she is referred to as being and as she pretends to be. It is difficult to imagine Mrs. Erlynne, with her inordinate respect for society, with her talent for flirtation and making the most of any situation, losing her self-possession in promiscuity. Her sexuality is all surface, as it is for all proper people in that society. We no more believe in her youthful passion than we do in Lady Windermere's passion although we can accept easily enough that both women are impulsively foolish.

After Ibsen, it is shocking to be thrown back into a world with the double standard. We can see the true dirtiness of this in Lord Windermere's response to Mrs. Erlynne when she is discovered in Lord Darlington's apartment. He has been decent to her previously, it is at once clear to us, not because he has accepted Mrs. Erlynne as a person in her own right whatever her past, but because he has been persuaded to believe that her past had been misrepresented. Lord Windermere is sufficiently emancipated to urge his wife to ignore social compulsion in inviting Mrs. Erlynne to their party, but his emancipation does not go far enough to allow to Mrs. Erlynne the same rights that he obviously allows to Lord Darlington or Lord Augustus. This pre-Ibsenian society, we must remember, is the one the principals are trying to claw their way into.

The final renunciation scene, which can so easily be read as melodrama, borders on the tragic, for we see plainly the possibilities the characters have for genuine, undirected response to one another. They are doomed to denying their feelings, doomed to destroying their identity as authentic individuals. Lord and Lady Windermere have their reputation to live up to; Mrs. Erlynne has hers to live down to. This society is as determining a force, as capricious and arbitrary, as regardless of worth and nobility and achievement, as indifferent to the individually human, as the fate of classical tragedy. And it destroys these persons no less thoroughly, consigning them to its own particular hell.

At first look Sean O'Casey strikes one as at the opposite pole from Wilde. Wilde wrote about aristocratic society, persons whose language was polished and witty, who never had to face the daily need of getting bread, lords and ladies who dressed in fashion and moved through fashionable settings. O'Casey, of course, wrote about proletarian society; his characters

speak with thick lower-class accents; they have no
taste in the furniture they buy or the clothes they
wear; they are oppressed by the need to make a living;
they are grubby, uncivilized, spontaneously emotional,
all the things Wilde's people are not. The differences
between O'Casey and Wilde may be multiplied many
times.

Yet there are points of contact. Perhaps most obviously both are very Irish—like Shaw and Synge and
Yeats—in their love of the well-turned phrase. Wilde's
idiom is certainly more polished, more neo-Classical
in its precision and balance; O'Casey's is Romantically self-indulgent, more concerned with feeling than
thought. Both approach the plausible excess of poetry.

More significantly, events in both are shaped by
politics, in Wilde by the politics of a specific society,
in O'Casey by the politics of a specific nation. And in
both the politics are particular and circumstantial, not
abstracted or universalized, so that we find in them a
highly patterned sociological texture very near the surface. Where Wilde is concerned with the smaller politics in his society that determine marriage, delineating
the maneuverings in endless detail, O'Casey is concerned with the politics of the dissolution of domesticity. Certainly family politics, the arrangements
involved in making and breaking marriages, stand
in relation to the larger politics of society as municipal
affairs stand in relation to national ones, the smaller
politics effected by the larger politics. And this is
exactly what we see in Wilde and in O'Casey. Lady
Bracknell's handling of the marriage of her daughter
to Jack Worthing is carried on in the context of the
demands of the larger society (the criteria she applies
to Jack and the list of eligible young men she has
made up are shared by other mothers in her set); the
marriages of the Boyles and of the Clitheroes break

up slowly under the variety of pressures of the Irish revolution.

But what connects Wilde and O'Casey most meaningfully is their tone of tragicomedy. The boredom and despair so evident throughout *The Importance of Being Earnest*, which reduces the bright young people to excesses of self-stimulus, which makes everyone frivolous about the only serious social gesture they all acknowledge, marriage, find their counterpart in O'Casey in the farcical collapses into primitive, infantile selfishness in the face of death, heroism, sacrifice. There are two levels of action in both, the serious one taken for granted by everyone, the one which gives energy to all activity and desire, and the one that mocks the serious one, that burlesques it, yet acknowledges its controlling importance by relating to it every gesture of slapstick, every thumbing of the nose. A critical difference may be discerned between Wilde and O'Casey, however, in their attitudes toward the serious level. Wilde's attitude toward it is so unfixed, ranging from respectful through ambivalent to contemptuous, that he very nearly obliterates that level.

But in O'Casey there is no doubt about the seriousness of the background. Jimmy Boyle cowers in the Boyle apartment, maimed and self-pitying, because he has betrayed a comrade; like his father he cannot live up to responsibility. A wildly farcical fight breaks out in the bar in *The Plough and the Stars* between two women, one of whom forgets the baby she has brought with her, at the same time as a rousingly patriotic demonstration is going on outside. While an Irish patriot is being dragged to safety, a bullet in his belly, the tenants of the apartment house go on an insane looting expedition, Mrs. Gogan returning with a chair on her head, Bessie Burgess with a baby carriage bulging with clothes, shoes, and a table.

O'Casey's terrible irony is hardly subtle. The irreducible meanness of people flashes out in the midst of heroism. Minnie Powell in *Shadow of a Gunman* risks her life for the poet not for reasons of patriotism, but because she has romantically convinced herself that he is a patriotic gunman, which he is too detached to be. Mrs. Grigson, in the same play, worried about her husband who has not come home on time, wonders whether "the insurance companies pay if a man is shot after curfew." "Isn't he a terrible man to be takin' such risks," she complains, "an' not knowin' what'll happen to him? He knows them Societies only wants an excuse to do people out of their money." Mrs. Gogan and Bessie Burgess, who have been arguing with each other like fishwives, agree that the dresses they have stolen ought to have the bodices raised so as to preserve the proprieties. Bessie Burgess is killed trying to save Nora Clitheroe surrounded by "a brass standard-lamp with a fancy shade" and "a vividly crimson silk dress, both of which have been looted."

O'Casey's landscape has nothing of Wilde's bleakness. His tragicomedy produces heroism out of farce as well as farce out of heroism. The Irish patriots may be driven as much by infantile fear and lust for glory as by principle, but it is Juno, amidst the farcical squalor of her household, who majestically dominates her surroundings even when she is at her nagging worst, like her Olympian namesake. Her son has met his shabby fate, compelled by treachery and vainglory, her husband has sunken into alcoholic bestiality; she goes out to raise a new family with her daughter, without men this time, not defeated in her hope that hearts of stone will turn to hearts of flesh.

Wilde's landscape, for all its dazzle and shine, is flat and barren. Before marriage there is the empty dance of Ernest; after, the fixed ritual of Lady Windermere; after marital crisis, the cynical arrangements of *An Ideal Husband* or *Lady Windermere's Fan*. Lady Windermere may be no less foolishly rigid in her patriotism to her society than Clitheroe is to his, but the results of her foolishness leave no serious flaw on the smooth terrain of her existence; Clitheroe's foolishness results in his death, Bessie's death, and his wife's madness. There is change, upheaval, a pulsating unexpectedness in O'Casey, testifying to possibility in human life. In O'Casey, weakness and strength have consequences that fill the landscape with shadows, with valleys and mountains.

The tragicomedy we find in Wilde and O'Casey is a characteristic tone in modern drama. Wilde's roots are not to be found altogether in Restoration comedy, for there the characters were in lusty, brutal attack on society; Wilde's comedy has more in common with the talky, sentimental work of Sheridan, whose characters acknowledged the dominance of society. But Wilde implicitly challenges his society by exaggerating its discourse into farce, its surface brightness into epigram, by emptying relationships of all content, by making content a matter of indifference. Wilde distorts, in short, in the manner of any caricaturist. His excess of playfulness becomes finally sad. When we encounter frustration and disappointment, boredom and melancholy, in the modern world, we do so often out of having too much of a good thing. Huysman's *Against the Grain* like Wilde's own *Dorian Gray* are studies in the tragedy of affluence.

In O'Casey, too, yielding too simply to possibility, accepting too readily the bravado of boasting and dreaming, leads to tragedy. It is as though Falstaff actually carried into reality his bombastic fictions, never pausing, as he reluctantly does, to accommodate them to the facts. O'Casey's people have the vitality of many of Shakespeare's lower-class characters, except that O'Casey puts them into a modern world where they themselves, and not their betters, must cope with the challenges of heroism. In O'Casey, we find both the horror and the grotesque comedy of modern gangsterism, a combination we also find in Brecht.

We are exposed to the epical gamut of human possibility in O'Casey, the range indeed of Homer and certainly of Brecht. One must linger on Bessie Burgess, for, like Achilles, she moves from the most vulgar, obscene pettiness to grandness. She is involved totally in slapstick at one moment, in heroism at another. Even Juno's domestic capaciousness, her protective understanding and vast acceptance, includes her waspishness of temper and vulgarity of taste. The poet in *Shadow of a Gunman* remains the poet, to be respected as such, in spite of his cowardice.

Clearly Wilde and O'Casey are not to be compared in terms of their intention or of their scope. Wilde's despair in his world was instinctive and, one would venture, unconscious; it never rose to the level of an informed bitterness. The tragicomedy in Wilde comes from his acceptance of his world as a man, an acceptance violated by his rejection of it as an artist, that is, as someone who must actually people that world with characters outside himself. Wilde's characters, like Wilde himself, build a vast defense system about themselves to survive; they even claim, like Wilde, to give their genius to living, only their talent to art. Certainly one must survive first as a man, which may well take the greater energy under some circumstances, to function as an artist. The seeming lack of heart in Wilde should be a sign for us, perhaps, of how much heart had to be expended in finding a way through the cold climates of Wilde's world. The impotent, strained joshing of Wilde's people, amiable though it is, is akin to the wisecracking that accompanies abandonment of hope.

Certainly O'Casey's conscious bitterness never descends to despair. Unlike Wilde, who finally saw little or nothing (although he apprehended much), O'Casey sees a great deal, the small and the large, foreground and background, the immediate and the remote. He combines and balances passion and detachment. He can lose himself in the description of a tenement or a saloon brawl, delighting in the details and character of the insults, but he also remains cool enough to relate these small tableaux to the vast ones of history. Unlike Joyce, who mixed his love for Ireland with his monumental and ego-centered contempt for it, O'Casey mixes with his anthropologically fine view of the Irish in place and time a deep and philosophical respect for all humanity, universal in its envelopment. The tragicomedy in O'Casey comes not from despair but from a full sense of the immense, the truly absurd, spread of man's possibility. Wilde's absurdity is miniaturistic; O'Casey's, gigantic.

In their quite different ways, Wilde and O'Casey set the tragicomic tone for later drama in the examination of man's relation to small world and large, to the total universe lying between paralysis and possibility.

6　MORAL PERSPECTIVE
IN PIRANDELLO

PIRANDELLO is first responded to in terms of his experimentalism, the *pirandellismo* which has made his name in the modern theater the counterpart of Joyce's in modern fiction, or of Yeats's in modern poetry. We do not normally and easily associate him with Ibsen or Shaw, theatrical innovators also, if not so daring or so philosophical in their innovations as Pirandello. We study Ibsen and Shaw in terms of their social import, the meaning first of all of their content. Yet Pirandello's experimentalism gains its force through his substance, the fabric of plot, theme, character; his manipulation of the conventional dramatic structure reinforces, is often identical with, his subject matter. *How* Pirandello says what he has to say is a good part of *what* he says. What Pirandello has to say is, finally, why he is worth considering at all in other than a purely historical and technical way.

Pirandello is not simply engaged in writing an endless essay on the tensions between art and reality. It is true that these tensions are of the essence in his "fantastic" plays, those based on some distortion of natural events (*Six Characters, It Is So! (If You Think So), Mountain Giants*), as well as of the "naturalistic" ones, in which there is no such distortion (*Liolà, Henry IV, Each In His Own Way, The New Col-*

ony, When Someone is Somebody). These tensions occupy Pirandello all the time, and it is obvious that in a general, philosophical way he is awed by the power of the opposition between art and reality, by the force binding the two. No matter how complicated a particular human situation becomes in his plays, at some point someone stops to remark on this tension. The Father in *Six Characters*, in the midst of defining and recreating his sticky domestic complication, assures the Director that he, the Father, as a character, is more "real" because of being fixed and unchanging, frozen in a moment of his career, than the Director who, being real, must constantly be changing from moment to moment, in a constant flux. Laudisi derisively closes each act of *It Is So! (If You Think So)* with his braying laugh deriding the effort to grasp truth. But this unrelenting insistence on the art-reality opposition is subordinate to moral matters and has final meaning, for that matter, in the context of highly particularized human situations.

It Is So! (If You Think So) illustrates the point. It is tempting to take this play as simply another little treatise in dramatic form on the nature of truth, on the difficulty of ever ascertaining it precisely. We have Laudisi's snickering refrain on truth, and of course the long discussions that precede and follow the several revelations of the plot, which are concerned with "truth," the question of who is really the mad one, Signora Frola, or her son-in-law, Signor Ponza.

And, indeed, the examination of the question of truth is charming, especially brilliant and lively, because it is so carefully embedded in the specific human arrangements of the drama. We are quite convinced, even if the people on the stage are not, of the slippery nature of truth, its relativity, its dependence on perspective, its detachment from mere fact (in the discussion about the documents, for example), and its final, impossible ambiguity (in Signora Ponza's declaration that she is both the daughter of Signora Frola *and* the second wife of Signor Ponza). Even more, we get a hint of one of Pirandello's major themes here: the unfixed state of truth in relation to the dramatic manipulation of it. For it is plain that both Signora Frola and Signor Ponza try to make a particular truth for the other. The "truths" they act out, while mutually exclusive, become the truths they live by; the truths become valid as the result of a conscious, controlled falsification.

Yet to take the play as only a treatise on truth is to fall into the same shortsighted and shallow intellectuality of the mob on the stage which is so intent on discovering the "truth." As the characters get involved in the triviality of the "plot," neglecting the human beings entangled in it, who are entangling themselves all the more out of desperation, so our involvement with the question of truth turns us away from what, in the first place, makes the whole question such a compelling one: the quite awful circumstances of Ponza and his wife and his mother-in-law. Becoming involved in the macabre comedy of the curiosity seekers, we neglect the tragedy of the Ponza ménage, the wiping out of so many members of the family by that earthquake, and the attempts at adjustment by the survivors. "Our feet are not quite on the ground," Signora Frola remarks pathetically. The complexity of the arrangements the three have worked out, a complexity that becomes fantastic, indicates how desperately they are trying to anchor themselves to some sort of reality and sanity, a sort where mere truth must allow itself to be shaped freely, in the service of a more compelling exigency. Even if Signora Frola and Signor Ponza are not, either one, "insane" about the

identity of Signora Ponza, the extravagant methodi-
calness of their juggling of truth—each pretending
madness to humor the other, for example; each offering identical explications for the behavior of the other
—suggests the extremities of thought and action to
which the two have been driven by the enormous
catastrophe which they have survived. Their art serves
their lives.

The horror which underlies the grotesque comedy
comes from the brutal, insatiable, but always well-
mannered prying of the officials of the town and their
ladies into the affairs of Ponza. They have been
begged by Signora Frola and Signor Ponza to leave
their private lives, however mysterious, alone, not by
either separately, it will be remembered, but by both.
The original, sympathetic concern with whether
Ponza is treating his mother-in-law humanely is
quickly replaced by a heartless curiosity, quite empty
of the impulse of charity, to uncover the mystery
which has prompted the Ponzas to arrange their cu-
rious affairs. Ponza is ready to give up his job to end
the campaign of inquiry which reaches the proportions of a lynching party in its lustfulness to resolve an
issue which is essentially trivial to the crowd—that
Ponza and his wife and mother-in-law are content in
their arrangement has long been established—but
which is of the essence of life-and-death to the principals involved. Ponza's cry of anguish to the crowd not
to pursue its investigation is unheeded. Ponza and his
mother-in-law, their intricately sustained charade exposed, leave the stage, defeated, weeping. Signora
Ponza, never unveiled, never identified, throws into
the crowd's teeth its own frivolous conundrum. Truth
is indeed a joke in the shadow of life.

Nor are the two tones of the play, the technical-
abstract and the living-human, to be separated, for the

essay on truth illuminates and is illuminated by the human agony. Truth emerges as less important than the need to accommodate to reality, in fact, as subservient to it, so subservient as to discard facts, less important facts (like documents proving identity) for more important ones (needs that are not to be denied or catalogued or compromised). The one truth finally accepted by everyone, explicitly by the Ponzas, implicitly by the onlookers, is that some kind of deal by the Ponzas with the demands of reality was justified in the light of their circumstances.

Truth, then, has meaning only in specific human terms, which always take precedence over the requirements of evidence, of philosophy, of cold intellectuality. But the tragedy here, as elsewhere, comes from the hubris of human beings who think they can long act out a truth detached from the facts, abstracted from them. And while our sympathies are certainly with the pathetic Ponzas, we must understand that the crowd in its fury embodies our own excessive respect for mere truth, it carries our own compelling curiosity about the details of abominations. To the degree that we are led to emphasize the discussion of truth in this play and to slight the details of the human tragedy, to that same degree may the crowd be justified in its thoughtless, unfeeling, inhuman passion.

SIGNORA SIRELLI   All you are saying is that we can never find out the truth! A dreadful idea! . . .

LAUDISI   . . . All I'm saying is that you should show some respect for what other people see and feel, even though it be the exact opposite of what you see and feel.

Truth without regard to its human embodiment is meaningless, as Laudisi keeps saying; yet the human situation which leaps away, for good reason or bad, from the roots of truth risks tragedy.

Surely the pathos of *It Is So (If You Think So)* is in part political. It would not be accurate to make the point too specific, that is, to relate the play to life under fascism; yet the pettiness of the gossip, the unfeeling disregard for privacy, the rationalization justifying the crowd's compulsion to know and to understand individual arrangements of individual needs, is a bitter comment on a society which takes as normal and necessary the flaying and dissection of persons moving on its fringe, unwilling or unable to participate in the ceremonies at the center. This is not the usual conformist lynching of nonconformists, which at least is done in the name of high principle; this is a dirty, gratuitous, unprincipled contempt for the private, differentiated human being. The hard, calculating searching here into the individual soul is akin to that depicted in *1984* and *Darkness at Noon*.

The Ponzas are unable, finally, to palm off their manipulation of truth on their society, and that is their tragedy. Liolà, however, manipulates truth successfully, and we have a sardonic comedy. The comedy of *Liolà* is not without its own bitter overtone, however, for playing with truth is never a harmless pastime. Uncle Simone, the old and sterile husband of Mita, is so blinded by his wish to think himself a father, that he is ready to accept any infant pressed on him as his own, accepting its mother also, and to cast out from his home his own wife for *her* sterility. The monomania of Uncle Simone, his senile nastiness, is sinister and unrelieved, unlike Liolà's equal monomania (to possess Mita, apparently the one eligible female in the Sicilian countryside who hasn't borne one of his bastards) which at least is modulated by a conscious sense of the absurd: his spelling out to Mita that the only way she can retain her reputable position as the wife of Uncle Simone's establishment is disreputably to yield to him, and offer to Simone as his own Liolà's inevitable offspring (Liolà has so firmly been established for us as a prodigious vehicle of fertility, there is no doubt that a pregnancy will occur).

We have, then at the end, Uncle Simone, triumphant in his self-delusion; Mita, sadly resigned in her triumph; and, finally, Liolà, symbolic of a literal creative impulse, leaving behind him, not just another infant, but a transformed situation, one shaped as much by his capacity for fertility as by his acumen in recognizing the human susceptibilities to manipulation. Liolà's shaping role is not unlike that of the playwright's, and it is rooted in a sensitive apprehension of the needs of people in particular situations, at particular times. Liolà, it should be emphasized, is never indifferent or irresponsible about the results of his creative realizations; he points out how thoroughly he has provided both psychic and physical security for his progeny. He acknowledges his responsibility as creator; he is concerned not only with *how* he carries off an action, but with *what* results from it. He does not, finally, separate style from matter.

In the sense of this recognition of his obligations, Liolà may be said to be more responsible than the author in *Six Characters in Search of an Author*, who created the characters and their situation and then, unable to resolve it, abandoned them to their fate. Of course, *Six Characters* is based on an absurdity, yet in spite of the clearly revealed and defined absurdity, the characters' insistence, for example, on their fixed and particularized lifelessness, we—and the actors, our representatives from the real world, on the stage—nevertheless are moved by the characters' living out their situation. For the characters permanently—and for the onlookers of the two audiences, the one on stage and the one in the theater, at least for the moment of the suspension of disbelief—the deaths at the final curtain are genuinely affecting. We are told that this is "mere" dramatization, as clearly as at any play when we watch the curtain go up, yet the double admonition of the play within the play does not release us from involvement. And we are not entirely released by the icy splash of the manager's quite sensible irritation: "Pretence? Reality? To hell with it all! Never in my life has such a thing happened to me. I've lost a whole day over these people, a whole day!" After all, the manager is engaged in the very practical, commercial, day-to-day activity of putting on plays, convincing audiences of the reality on the stage; what has he to do with allowing himself to become convinced of a reality created there before his eyes by disembodied characters, acting under the impulse of an absent and irresponsible author? He, indeed, proves himself unreal by rejecting his normal human response to the deaths.

The infinite flux and infinite shaping potential of all contrived and controlled action, the infinite possibilities of response, especially of actors trained to simulate and dissemble, and consequently professionally subject to changes of feeling and thought, are explored in *Each In His Own Way*, with its series of stages receding into infinity, like images in a barber shop which has mirrors on all the walls. We in the seats of the theater respond to the responses of an audience sitting up there on the stage, who discuss their responses to the play they are watching, which is the same one we see. And within the action of the play, which both audiences are watching, are additional audiences and stages: the first scene takes place in an anteroom, to the rear of which a party is going on; guests drift in and out of the party and exchange comments in the anteroom "lobby" about the action going on at the party. Diego repeatedly assumes a stage with his passionate and obscure dramatic monologues, in the very moment of holding his audience's attention (and ours) making a point of the persuasive power of dramatic statement. (Surely the piling on of theatrical tricks here becomes other than a trick itself, becomes a statement of theme?)

Against this background of delightfully playful, ingenious machinery, which tickles us by itself, is set an involved, extravagant, melodramatic love affair, the "real" principals of which are in the stage audience, the depicted principals of which are in the stage play. The play itself, like all plays within plays since Hamlet's production of the murder of Gonzago, is somewhat tedious, talky, dull, but, as with Hamlet's play, the point is not what happens on the stage, but the effect of that on the audience. And, of course, Delia Moreno, the "real" actress in the stage audience, finds herself compelled to respond to her "real" lover, also in the audience, in the same way that Delia Morello, who depicts her in the play play, responds to *her* stage lover. We, in the audience audience, watch a created action flow over the footlights. We see how drama determines and is determined by life; we see how helpless one can be against the power of drama, for we are made helpless ourselves.

While only particular persons are engulfed by this overflow of drama into life, in terms of the particular situation dramatized, we, the innocent bystanders, are not left untouched. For a significant point is made very early in the play, long before the two separate worlds of stage and audience coalesce. Delia Morello, the actress in the play play, comes to thank Doro for his defence of her during the trivial party argument

that started the action. "The fact is," she says to
Doro, "that what you said of me suddenly made me
see myself." "Ah," says Doro, "so then I guessed
right." "As right," replies Delia, "as though you had
lived my life to the bottom . . . but understanding
me in a way I had never understood myself! Never!
Never! And you can't imagine with what joy and with
what anguish I recognized myself, saw myself . . . in
all the things you found to say of me!"

Delia, then, a professional actress, needs a critical
guide to understand herself, and she is ready to flit
from one explanation to another. Her activities are
subject to opposing interpretations, each plausible,
and each, indeed, assumed by the two young antago-
nists, as each is persuaded by the other.

"All our ideas," says Diego, "change in the restless
turmoil we call life. We think we catch a glimpse of a
situation! But let us just discover something contrary
to what we thought! So-and-so was a white man, eh?
Well, at once he's a black man."

We, in the audience audience, like those in the
stage audience, are worked on by drama to change
both ideas and emotions, even to absorb new ones, to
become other than what we were before our exposure
to the play.

But, again (as in *It Is So!* and in *Liolà*), Pirandello's sympathies, our sympathies, are finally with the
driven persons, with those who must live with the
absurdity of a passionate, mercurial impressionable-
ness, which, on a lower level, impels sincere and serious
young men to a duel, both verbal and actual, and on a
more intense level, impels the actress and her lover to
succumb to the agony of their disastrous alliance. The
members of the stage audience in the stage lobby
murmur about the impropriety of reflecting sensa-
tional reality on the stage, and some of them mutter

imprecations against the riddles of Pirandello, but when the dramatic action explodes into the lobby, they look and listen with the same obscene and unconfused attentiveness that marks the human pack in *It Is So!*

When we see in Pirandello an audience on the stage reacting to an action, we are seeing an extension of ourselves: it is we who are involved in the action, affecting it, absorbing it. For Pirandello, drama is more than imitation of an action, it is, equally, response to an action. One production of *Each in His Own Way* put the stage audience into the real audience, emphasizing this continuity. It may have been a farcical underlining of this continuity when a member of the real audience, responding to the stage manager's apology closing the play after two apparent acts, indignantly demanded a refund of his admission, but this is the sort of union of the play world with the real world that a Pirandello play insists upon.

Pirandello's main question as a philosopher is with the interrelation of these two worlds, and as an author is with the possibility of manipulating either of these worlds with relation to the other, of modulating and changing one or the other. In *Henry IV*, this conscious control of the external world is contracted to the situation of an individual alone. Henry IV's madness is as ambiguously methodical as Hamlet's. Henry IV is the chief actor in a production he has written and is still directing, and he is no more mad than Hamlet was (who was also a play director, of course), or than his friends and their friends who conform to his costume and court, and no more sane than any actor who can persuade himself, however momentarily, or allow himself not to doubt, that he is indeed the character he portrays. Henry IV's need is not less than the Ponzas' need even though it is more special, more limited, more weakly motivated. His masquerade may be even more desperately rooted in the need to insulate himself from the outside world, for he does kill a man in the brief moment when he unmasks himself and returns to reality. The Ponzas may, after all, work out still another accommodation to still another outrage committed against them. Playing on the border between the real and the false cannot be casual.

When Someone is Somebody has such a poignantly autobiographical overtone that it very nearly does not make its point with the same universal application as *It Is So!* or *Henry IV*. Delago, the young poet created by XXX, the distinguished literary Someone of the play, complete with a body of work, does not really appear in his own person even though Veroccia, his young mistress, is present. We do not see XXX as Delago, even with Veroccia; he talks even with her of his life as XXX. Pirandello avoids the temptation of expressionism. XXX does not sit at his desk, a manikin with a phonograph in his stomach, as he speaks of doing, but he does become a statue of himself at the final curtain, a marble prisoner of his fate. The tragedy of XXX is that he cannot turn drama to his needs, that with all his artistry, he remains XXX and cannot become someone else, a refugee from his fate, even for a moment, like Ponza.

The Mountain Giants, undoubtedly Pirandello's most ambitious play, which unhappily was not finished, is in the nature of a response to the conclusions of *When Someone is Somebody* and even to *The New Colony*, the depiction of an unsuccessful Utopian attempt. Cotrone, the Magician, speaks: "If you still view life within the limits of the natural or of the possible, Countess, I warn you that you will never understand a thing out here. We are now outside these limits, thank God. All we have to do is imagine, and our imagination instantly takes on life, by itself."

The settlers in *The New Colony* worked within the limits of the natural and the possible, and consequently were doomed. The great writer, finally, was trapped also by the barriers of the natural and possible; his creation, Delago, was quite natural and possible, if unlikely. The natural and possible, however far stretched, will bounce back furiously. The Ponzas worked on its borders, never overstepping them, and were very nearly destroyed before the play ends, and very possibly totally destroyed after unless they finally did transcend these borders: how can one continue to live long within the natural and possible with Signora Ponza's assertion that she is simultaneously two different persons?

Who then can transform the disasters, the momentary ones as well as the eternal and monstrous ones, inherent in the natural and possible? Pirandello's answer is unequivocal. "Only poets can give coherence to dreams," says Cotrone, the Magician. We on the mountain, says Cotrone, "believe in the reality of ghosts more than in that of bodies."

What is the problem then? Why could not the Ponzas carry off their elaborate dramatic production, why couldn't Someone become someone else other than Somebody? Why cannot the powers of poetry, of art, prevail and extend our territory for living beyond the natural and possible? Pirandello, living in a society where art was confined, gives us a pessimistic answer. Both the upholders of the natural and possible as well as the magical makers of the unnatural and impossible are to blame for our unsatisfactory answers to these questions. Stefano Pirandello, on the basis of conversations with his father, recounts the conclusion to *The Mountain Giants*. The actress is destroyed by the people, broken like a puppet. The actors who come to her defence are torn to pieces.

Pirandello's sense of the absurdity and bleakness of the contemporary human situation is relieved only by his sympathy with any attempts to escape it or to mitigate it. Efforts like those of the Ponzas and of Henry IV, however foredoomed they may be because of the unyielding demands made by the natural and possible, are at least heroic, for the human imagination is involved at its highest manifestation, creativity. Pirandello very nearly applauds the attempts although, with a hard sense of the inevitable, he does not bemoan the failure. An attempt like that in *The New Colony* to make a society on the basis of some poor-spirited urge to escape, not through the imagination but through a mundane logic, is worthless, having as its aim a duplication in microcosm of the mainland; it is doomed to sink into the sea, an ending prophesied but ignored because of the incapacity of the imagination to envisage the possibility.

Pirandello recognizes that the dramatic may be a way not only for a momentary accommodation to the abominations of life but also for a more permanent accommodation, that is, an understanding recognizing the infinitely reciprocating effects between art and reality. The responsibility may be best exercised, as it was not in *It Is So!*, through the nearly active and certainly *sympathetic* participation of the observer in the created dramatic situation he makes himself party to.

We acknowledge the power of drama simply by going to the theater, reading a play, ready to allow ourselves to be persuaded. Pirandello insists that ultimately this is a moral power and that this power is shared by us with the makers of drama: we submit to becoming participants in human affairs. We bear responsibility with the playwright (and director, and actors, *et al.*). We have the burden of bringing a serious and sensitive receptivity to the created thing, of enabling the poet to make contact with us, helping him with our readiness to mesh the natural-and-possible with the unnatural-and-impossible. Pirandello's very great and unique achievement was to make this union himself at every moment, in every play, and to do so with an unflagging moral intention.

THE MORALITY OF PASSION:
        LORCA'S THREE TRAGEDIES

WITH LORCA we enter an altogether different landscape
in the modern drama, the landscape of passion. His
three great tragedies—*Blood Wedding, Yerma, The
House of Bernarda Alba*—are stripped nearly bare of
the details of setting and time, that sense of locale we
need for Ibsen, Wilde, Shaw, or O'Casey. Yet we do
not leave the area of reality, as we do with some of
Strindberg and of Pirandello. Lorca empties his drama
of nearly all forces but passion. Even his settings always seem nearly barren, simply all whites or all
blacks, so that only the colors emerge that are evoked
by the action and the characters. The motivation and
energy for plot are in passion; the definition of character is through passion. There is no "thought," no
"idea" of any significance.

Lorca is preeminently the playwright of passion in
the modern theater although we can find elements of
Lorca in Williams, Osborne, O'Neill, and Genet; but
in each of these there is a significant admixture of
other thematic material. Lorca's passion is not related
to a program, as in D. H. Lawrence, or in Williams, or
in Genet. Lorca's "blood consciousness" is a consciousness of what is, already; of what must be ob-
served, acknowledged, assimilated, lived with, understood, and, finally, even forgiven. Lorca's passion is

rooted in an established social context. The tragedy in his plays comes from the tension between passion, which is necessarily always entirely individual and personal and whimsical, and the society in which the individuals move, which defines them and also gives a particular value and shading to passion and its manifestations. In Lorca, the conflict is between passion and honor, where passion is the mark of the personal (willful and private and powerful in its needs) and honor that of the social (rigid and public and equally powerful in its rules and taboos, the denial of needs).

Blood Wedding offers a bare plot, as spare as a scenario for a ballet, nearly melodramatic in its familiarity and excesses, but only as a skeletal structure to enclose the several domains of passion which combine to give the play its enormous intensity and energy.

The passion of the Mother is both personal and general, her own particular agony enlarged to the dimensions of universal maternal passion. The play opens immediately with a clear indication of the boundaries of maternal passion: her sense of loss of her husband and son is separate and different from her surviving son's sense of loss of father and brother. Throughout the play she continues to define herself as a widow and bereaved mother. At one point, she asks "Can you really see me? Don't I seem mad to you?" That is, does she have an existence outside her loss of husband and son. When she speaks to her son, the Bridegroom, about how to treat his wife, she evokes again the memory of her lost husband, having learned about such matters, she says, from him.

But it is not passion alone which defines the Mother, either as an individual or as a force. It is also honor. Mothers live not only in family but also in society. Honor and passion mingle in the mother to nourish her growing lust for vengeance. And at the end of the play it is her fulfilled but terribly thwarted passion that comes to match and balance the terribly unfulfilled *potential* passion of the bride, who will never be wife or mother and has not even been a beloved, except in hope.

Maternal passion has its domain in the heart of proper society. The other pole of passion in *Blood Wedding* is that of the lovers, outside that society. The lovers are awed by the passion they rouse in themselves. Leonardo says: "To burn with desire and keep quiet about it is the greatest punishment we can bring on ourselves." And the Bride replies a little later: "And I know I'm crazy and I know my breast rots with longing; but here I am. . . ." And in her final self-justification, to the mother of the Bridegroom she betrayed:

> You would have gone, too. I was a woman burning with desire, full of sores inside and out, and your son was a little bit of water from which I hoped for children, land, health; but the other one was a dark river, choked with brush, that brought near me the undertone of its rushes and its whispered song. And I went along with your son who was like a little boy of cold water—and the other sent against me hundreds of birds who got in my way and left white frost on my wounds, my wounds of a poor withered woman, of a girl caressed by fire. I didn't want to; remember that! I didn't want to. Your son was my destiny and I have not betrayed him, but the other one's arm dragged me along like the pull of the sea, like the head toss of a mule, and he would have dragged me always, always, always—even if I were an old woman and all your son's sons held me by the hair!

The Bride insists to the Mother: "You would have gone, too." That is, "You who know what it is to act on passion would have gone, too."

When they are alone in the woods, an area set off

from the everyday world, the lovers are very conscious
of how their passion appears to that world. The bride
refers to herself as a bitch. "I, too," says Leonardo to
her, "would want to leave you if I thought as men
should." But the passion that provides the energy to
break through the barriers of honor, to get outside the
walls of society, must be as great as it is illicit. It must
in its intensity equal the passion of the mother; the
passion of vice must balance the passion of virtue.

Passion, then, in Lorca has strength to form its own
moral universe. Tragedy comes when this new universe of passion must be opposed by the larger and
older universe of logic, of order, of society. The opposition is stated now prosaically, now lyrically, from the
center of the passionate universe (the lovers), from
outside it (the Woodcutters, who remind one of the
detached gravediggers in *Hamlet*): "You have to follow your passion," one says, "They did right to run
away." But what must necessarily happen, as it happens in *Romeo and Juliet*, is that passion unrooted in
an ordered universe cannot survive beyond the initial
momentum. It can only frustrate ironically. Everyone
in *Blood Wedding* is left bereft, although the Bride
seems most punished. The Mother has been a wife
and mother and she has had a measure of vengeance.
The Bride must go on living as a woman who has
destroyed both husband and lover through passion.

Yerma's life shadows the life of the Bride: if the
Bride had not fled with Leonardo, she might have
found herself a Yerma. Yerma does not love her husband. She has no pleasure in her emotional life; there
is only a flicker of response, empty as a conventional
flirtatious gesture or intonation, in her contact with
another man than her husband. She has so turned
inward she has no capacity to feel normally. She is
admonished at one point by an old woman: "Men

have got to give us pleasure, girl." But her only impulse toward pleasure is maternal. Her wish to be a mother is hysterical in its excess, and perhaps, thus, self-defeating because it does not accommodate calmly and compromisingly to the possibilities. (One has to think only of how Mita solved her problem in Pirandello's *Liolà*, also a folk drama, to recognize the potential immediacy of Yerma's salvation.)

It is properly not clear from the text whether Yerma or her husband is infertile. It is clear that Yerma has lost the capacity to make union, to give herself in passion to a man, specifically to her husband, but also, as the old women who hover about the action of the play suggest, to any man. Yerma is limited by the demands of honor, the established social ritual, in working out her maternal drive. One old woman says flatly that only men can help Yerma, although she is willing to try black magic: witches, the supernatural, come more within the proper social limits than adultery. Unable to break out of her armor of honor, fashioned by the passion of her own regard for society, she turns her passion inward. She speaks of becoming her own son; she addresses her body; she describes herself as being on the edge of sanity.

Yerma's passion in a sense has less to do with maternity than with sheer fertility. Becoming a mother, that act alone, isolated from the biological and emotional realities, seems to be enough to fulfill her passion. "For I'm hurt, hurt and humiliated beyond endurance," she says, "seeing the wheat ripening, the fountains never ceasing to give water, the sheep bearing hundreds of lambs, the she-dogs; until it seems the whole countryside rises to show me its tender sleeping young, while I feel two hammer-blows here, instead of the mouth of my child." Juan, her husband is himself not interested in passion, merely the sensual; he is

phlegmatic and resigned: wearing himself out physically seems to be equal for him to fulfilling himself
physically. He has not the vitality in any case to rouse
himself to the pitch of passion that Yerma requires,
and it is poetically just, if ironic, for Yerma to murder
him at last, to take out her frustrated passion, so to
speak, against the frustrator, thus once and for all
eliminating any possibility to have her need for maternity "honorably" satisfied.

Murder is scarcely more honorable than adultery, of
course: if Yerma is finally to find power to pierce her
armor of honor, she might have found a lover to
father her child. But Yerma has gone far out of the
territory of the reasonable or plausible, driven by her
inner and constrained by her outer passion. She has
entered a mad, surrealistic landscape, where murder
and motherhood, destruction and creation, sterility
and fertility, become equated because exactly opposite, exactly self-cancelling.

In *The House of Bernarda Alba*, we have what
amounts to a nunnery and all that implies of the
suppression of passion: nunneries are refuges from the
usual passion of the world. Bernarda Alba is sadisti-
cally compulsive about order, pathological about
cleanliness. As in *Yerma*, in which the two old maids
spend all their time keeping their house spotless, so
the barrenness, immaculateness of Bernarda Alba's
establishment are related to sterility; her house is not
merely a denial of passion but a denigration of it.
Bernarda, loudly: "Magdalena, don't cry. If you want
to cry, get under your bed."

We remember that in *Blood Wedding*, Leonardo
lives a "disordered" life: he cannot hold down a job,
he is hot-tempered and impatient, he comes from a
line of murderers. He is thematically equated with a
wild stallion. But none of this is pejorative, merely

descriptive; Leonardo is of that world where violence alone is heroic. The Bridegroom represents order, cleanliness, and wealth. Bernarda Alba is rich and viciously opposed to irregular emotions: "Hot coals in the place where she sinned," she screams horribly about the local girl who has given herself to a number of men. As we hear the threat of the galloping stallion in *Blood Wedding*, threatening the orderly arrangement of events, so one hears the hoofbeats of the caged animal in *Bernarda Alba*, a tattoo of threatening disaster again.

Bernarda Alba is an extreme distillation of social honor; she exemplifies a passion that has gone too far in excluding the mortally impulsive, irrational, emotional, self-indulgent. It has become in its extremity antipassion. When one daughter says, "I should be happy, but I'm not," Bernarda Alba replies, "It's all the same." (Of course, it's not all the same, not even for Bernarda, as her frenzy to undo things at the end of the play testifies.) In effect, Bernarda is a Satanic spirit, living in an atmosphere of death, perversion, and denial. The play starts with a funeral and ends with a suicide; between we have sadism, insanity, onanism. There are black curtains on the windows. Sexual passions are outside this territory: the stallion drumming in his stall; the village escapades. No men appear on stage. The setting is on the edge of action. The only action that occasionally can burst out in Bernarda Alba's house is the poultrylike squabbling of the sisters, a parody of life.

In *The House of Bernarda Alba*, then, we get an extended examination of the pathology of social passion, of an honor that is contemptuous of the individually human, that is, finally, self-defeating. Bernarda Alba did bear five children, but we are to gather that this was in the cause of social honor, that whatever

private passion she might have begun with has attenuated into nothingness, been distorted into self-ha-
tred. She hates her daughters. Bernarda Alba's passion
is exercised in the extinguishing of passion: the sadist
can only have definition through the masochist, his
diametrical opposite. As the play opens, we see Bernarda Alba finally retiring into the "ideal" existence,
waiting primly for death, her social duties done, indifferent to the suppressed but smoldering vitality of
the unattached daughters. Bernarda Alba fears and
hates sex in any form, for sex means only life.

The conclusion of *Bernarda Alba* crystallizes earlier
thematic hints and motifs. Adela hangs herself on
learning, mistakenly, that her lover has been killed. In
a veritable hysteria, Bernarda Alba shrieks that Adela
died a virgin, forbids tears except in private, and calls
for silence, silence, silence, as the curtain descends.
Cleanliness, purity, silence, defining marks of death
itself, envelope Bernarda Alba's house. "Death must
be looked at face to face," she pronounces as Adela's
body is cut down.

In *Blood Wedding*, the tragedy develops from the
opposed passions of the lovers and those of the world
they move in; the forces are embodied in Leonardo on
one side, in the mother on the other. But there is a
continuum in passion; it comes full circle, wherever it
may start. The text opens with a chilling litany by the
Mother about knives ("Cursed be all knives. . . . everything that can slice a man's body") and closes with
the Mother and Bride chanting alternately about "a
tiny knife/ that barely fits the hand,/ but that slides
in clean/ through the astonished flesh/ and stops at
the place/ where trembles, enmeshed,/ the dark root
of a scream." Initially impelled by opposing passions,
the Mother and the Bride are joined together in the
common passion of bereavement: passion becomes a

moral force for making the human experience, wherever it may start, a final common and vital one, enclosing all possibilities, including conflicting ones.

In *Yerma*, we do not have external oppositions; Yerma herself encloses the opposites that destroy her: passion and honor themselves unwind the tragedy in her, her own passion, her own honor, both too great to yield or accommodate to the other. Her individual, nearly maniacal impulse toward motherhood, so private, so violent, is not less than her obsessed sense of her place in society, even when the evidence is offered to her of the death implicit in proper sterility. Like Lady Macbeth, she rises steadily to a height of mania, oppressed by the too great burden of reconciling private need with public prohibition. She breaks, and in breaking is finally freed of the restraints of taboo; self-abandoned, she murders, fulfilling at last, while utterly cancelling, her private passion. Honor finally asserts its own passionate power.

Bernarda Alba climaxes this trilogy of the tragedy of passion by seeming to assert that it is "honor," passion perverted by a sense of the social that excludes the human, which somehow survives and even triumphs, however abominably, over the personal passion. We may thus read these tragedies as concluding on a pessimistic note: the world of Bernarda Alba is one in which human impulses may not range freely, must be constrained, even expunged, even at the risk of the ugliest consequences, of perversions of passion and of life, including madness, self-stimulation, torture, suicide. But the very extremity of this view suggests its own rebuttal; Bernarda Alba's mode cannot sustain itself except by a restlessly conscious, eternally remorseless exercise of death-dealing. The professional murderer himself dies a measure with each death he arranges. The Nazis, the hired hands of Murder, Inc.,

Bernarda Alba act out a slow suicide. But the victims, whatever the intimidation, unless they conspire in their own long day's dying, hold on to life, one way or another. Even as Bernarda Alba is hysterically improvising her sterile stagecraft for the future, managing the appearance of Adela's suicide ("Take her to another room and dress her as though she were a virgin"), arranging to face death daily, another daughter, Martirio, mutters: "A thousand times happy she, who had him." (For every Eichman there is a Bruno Bettelheim, more than one, to man's glory.) The personal, physical passion continues to assert its independent power. Honor may finally turn to antipassion, as in Bernarda Alba, certainly with its own power, but the primal force is personal passion.

Lorca's tragedy, then, resides in the domain of passion: passion destroys itself and its possessors, the personal can ultimately only come in conflict with the social, the social enlarges itself into vengeance or into death-serving sterility. Life and fulfillment may reside in passion alone, but precariously, never without risk, not casually. Humans cannot truly be alive without passion, but with passion they must wage a running, alert, and subtle battle with those guerilla forces intent on its destruction. It is the classic opposition between life and death itself; and death, of course, as Freud not least has sadly indicated, is an expression, a wish, of life itself. But to celebrate passion is to celebrate life, living, feeling, reaching, erring: vitality, vivacity, whimsicality, impulsiveness, energy of every sort. There is a final rightness about Lorca's characters who strive toward goals that define them as they live, as there is about Oedipus, and to fail is simply—and greatly—to be human.

IT IS PERHAPS unfortunate that the revival of interest
in the United States in Bertolt Brecht came about, in
part, through the Off Broadway adaptation of *The
Three Penny Opera*. While the basic plot of the original was left more or less intact, the Théâtre de Lys
production made the details nearly pretty, prettier
even than those in John O'Hara's *Pal Joey*, perhaps
the closest American counterpart. Joey is a gigolo, and
Mac the Knife in Brecht's original is a pimp, rapist,
and murderer. But in the adaptation, we never quite
find out what Mac's vocation is and what his avoca-
tion; he is a generalized and romanticized "bad guy."
We are reluctant to accept the viciousness of Brecht's
original, and we insulate ourselves from it.

If we had come to Brecht in something of his un-
distilled original quality, we may have been more
ready to see American social drama in a larger perspective. The failures and the successes particularly of
Odets, Hellman, and Miller, but also of the "proletarian" drama of the thirties, may with peculiar revelation be examined against the background of Brecht's
particular attack on not dissimilar problems.

Brecht was involved, whatever else he committed
himself to, in an examination of human depravity
anywhere while trying to find sufficient decency some-

where to make life minimally tolerable. In this he was like Freud, who started as a physician of the sick and awful in the individual and became a moralist concerned with man. One or two of Brecht's plays may even be read as schematically Freudian. *The Good Woman of Setzuan,* for example, is very much a morality play about the schizoid balance involved in survival: idealism vs. accommodation, good vs. evil. The moving action involves a split: "the injunction to be good and yet to live. . . . I could not do it." This is the theme: how to be good in the world, yet good to oneself: how to be both moralist and egoist, how to satisfy both self and conscience, both ego and super-ego.

Setting in Brecht is unrealistic or irrelevant; his China is not any real China, the stockyards are not Chicago. He was concerned with allegorical landscapes, with jungles, which loom as ideas. No matter how specific a situation, Brecht transcended it. *Mother Courage* takes place, "fantastically" of course, over a panorama of time and space: it is an "epic" of a mother, her attempts to survive and protect her family not in the context of any specific war but in that of war in general, and, by extension, in the context of all catastrophe. She improvises endlessly, working with whatever of the human residuum she finds at hand, keeping her identity in disaster. Like Bettelheim in the concentration camps, she survives by the constant study of how one survives, salvaging identity through studying and exercising identity.

St. Joan of the Stockyards is more profitably compared with *Major Barbara* (with which it has all sorts of parallels) rather than with, say, Wexley's *They Shall Not Die,* about the Scottsboro boys, an anticapitalist play. Like *Major Barbara,* *St. Joan of the Stockyards* is allegorical; like *Major Barbara,* it is a study of innocence turning into experience, sophistication, and finally cynicism, in a modern setting of giant industrialism. The millionaires in Brecht who manipulate the stock market, a little like Andrew Undershaft, alternate between being viciously hard and being sentimental. Joan herself, Salvation Army lass, is not attractive: her naiveté is charming but also dense and willful. The tone, as in O'Casey, is Homeric; we see the pettiness of personages whose affairs control the lives of hundreds of thousands. We see that frivolous selfishness is woven through the totality of the human fabric, as when the militant wife of the worker who was caught in the grinding machine is bought off with a meal ticket at the plant commissary.

Brecht always leaped quickly from the particular to the general. American social playwrights, on the other hand, preferred documentary of one sort or another, an authenticity of time and place, a "consistent" characterization of good and evil, a clear line between victim and oppressor, and we can see by contrast with Brecht how constricted or distorted the results were. From Brecht—through Hellman and Odets—to Miller there has been a steady movement away from the social context in its allegorical dimension to an emphasis on the individual and personal as almost to obscure, certainly to confuse, the social issue.

The Hubbards of Hellman's *The Little Foxes* are portrayed in the bold strokes of caricature: they don't speak civilized English; they are greedy; selfish, even with one another; cruel to the point of sadism, dishonest, anti-Negro; etc.; etc. Whatever is bad about big bad American capitalists is especially vicious and villainous in the Hubbards of the Deep South. So far this might be the start of a Brechtian situation, but the picture gets blurred by the details.

The vulgarity of the Hubbards is contrasted, first,

with the sensitivity and refinement of Birdie, a Hub-
bard only by marriage, who once owned a great, white,
lovely plantation where Negroes were thoughtfully
cared for, and second, with that of Mr. Marshall from
Chicago, who sees through the grasping vulgarity of
the Hubbards. Regina's masculinity and frigidity, especially, are opposed to Birdie's fluttering femininity.
Are we to infer—or sense—that there was something
essentially feminine about the antebellum South and
that there is something essentially asexual, bitchy, sadistic about the new ruling class? As for Marshall, a
gentleman of poise, decency, gentleness, urbanity, sophistication—everything, in short, the Hubbards are
not—does he not set into motion the whole enterprise
of the Hubbards? He flirts sexually with Regina as he
flirts commercially with her brothers. As a capitalist,
he is no less guilty of the whole machination than the
Hubbards themselves; he may, according to the rules
of good old-fashioned morality, even be more guilty,
for he consciously uses them to do his own dirty work.

Regina is at the heart of the play; it is a role for a
grand leading lady. The musical play based on *The
Little Foxes* is called *Regina*. Regina is a woman
much like Hedda Gabler. Is Regina's problem personal or social? She is ready to sell her daughter, to
give up everything for what she wants. Unlike Hedda,
she has been married to an intelligent, genuinely aristocratic man. But she is driven by a lustful and entirely private restlessness. She says to her daughter:
"Somewhere there has to be what I want." Only at
the end of the play does she reveal herself without her
armor, making, briefly and tangentially, the kind of
justification for herself that Hedda more consciously
makes. And suddenly we wonder whether she may
not have been involved in more than a scheme to
exploit poor Negroes and poor Whites. She may have

been involved, indeed like Hedda, in a process of self-discovery, self-definition, in trying to live, within the limits of her capacity, a richer life than her present, plainly constricting one. This emergence of the private, merely whimsical, accidental character of Regina blunts the social point of the play. In Brecht's *St. Joan*, capitalism rots the souls of all classes; we waste no time ruminating on the private psyches of workers or bosses.

Watch on the Rhine obscures its anti-Nazi message even more strikingly. It describes the coming of the anti-Nazi underground to the United States in terms of the visit of a leader of that underground to the Washington, D. C., home of his in-laws. The in-laws, the Farrellys, stand for traditional American decency, all the way back to the Adams family. At this hallowed shrine of American decency, two men meet, Kurt Müller, representing the anti-Nazi underground, and Teck de Brancovis, representing the forces of indecency. The point is hammered at us that "the watch on the Rhine," the sentinel posts guarding against the invasion by the legions of indecency, may be found right in Washington; it is not a battle taking place somewhere else but is right here with us, on the Potomac, involving everyone.

But a number of questions arise. Why does Kurt travel around with his wife and children (except to prepare us for his melodramatic leavetaking)? The commands to his son to care for the family are intended mainly to involve us emotionally. Any sensible, practical underground man would have arranged for such details earlier and otherwise. Can we altogether accept the Farrellys becoming accessories to murder, the most extreme violation of the communal law of their society? Can we altogether believe in Kurt Müller himself, who is not merely too good to be true, so to speak, a man committed to martyrdom, but who betrays streaks of plain masochism in his heroic posing? Why are all the characters so familiar: the gruff but really soft-hearted dowager; the faithful, sacrificing, dry-eyed wife; the doll-like children?

Where we have caricatures in *The Little Foxes*, we have stereotypes in *Watch on the Rhine*. The whole play and the characters are presented with a handsome skill, to be sure, so handsome as almost to keep us from suspending our skepticism about the trite and in the well-made. But only for the moment and especially when placed side by side with Brecht.

How might Brecht have handled the characters? We have evidence. Mother Courage conveys the quality of maternity so much more convincingly than Sara Müller perhaps precisely because she is a parody of the eternal Mother, because she is, simply, true (true, perhaps, only through distortion): vulgar, shrill, unexpectedly tender, always improvising in the interest of her maternity. Mother Courage is an epic, a panoramic mother; Sara Müller is a miniaturized, particularized, anecdotal one. Galileo, also truly heroic, is an exasperatingly real man, on whom heroism is thrust, to whom sought after heroism would seem only farcical, self-denying.

Brecht might have had the children in *Watch on the Rhine* carrying messages; he might have given them knives and pistols to use (consider the ironic familial relations in *Three Penny Opera*); they would have been at least realistically bratty. Hellman is to Brecht as Russian "social realism" in painting is to Grosz or Kollwitz. Hellman is writing for a mass audience that has expectations regarding heroic fathers, mothers, and children, that has been conditioned to expect of dowagers certain speech and behavior. She even uses that audience's expectation that murder be always punished to make the point that killing a Nazi sympathizer (or even agent) without trial in Washington is not really murder at all.

The familial situation in Odets's *Awake and Sing* becomes so energized by its independent intention that the ostensible theme of the play is obscured. Instead of remaining a study of the disintegration of a family by the forces of the Depression, the play becomes a study in the systematic emasculation of the male members of a Jewish family by a typical Jewish mother, a situation that might take place anytime. Bessie recognizes something of the sort herself when she describes her role: "I am both father and mother." But unlike the hermaphroditic good person of Setzuan, she is both male and female not in her dealing with society but in handling her family. She works in a factory to send her husband to law school. She uses her martyrdom (a little like Müller) to whine her way into cowing everyone around her. When Ralphie complains about never having had roller skates like other children, she argues him down with the reminder that he always had the "best specialists" when he was sick. (But why was he always sick? A sick child, as they say, is a dependent one.) Bessie keeps books on her sacrifices: the parallel columns show how much more she did for her family than other mothers did for theirs. Her excessive pride in her children's cleanliness is self-pride.

Who does not succumb to Bessie? The venal capitalist, not worthy of being benefited by Bessie's maternal protectiveness, and the man who may be said to have already been symbolically castrated by society and so earned the right to independence, the man with one leg. The decent persons are all lost, but it is obvious that it is not simply the Depression which has cast them into hell: it is Bessie using the Depression.

The "typical" mother in immigrant Jewish family life in America in the twenties and thirties *needed* to be needed. Fortunately for her (and for Odets, in *Awake and Sing*), the Depression provided a more than adequate opportunity to satisfy this need as it stripped men of their jobs and forced them to spend their days around the kitchen. *Awake and Sing*, about a Jewish matriarchal family in the America of the Depression, is like *Juno and the Paycock*, a play about an Irish matriarchal family during deprivation and rebellion. But where O'Casey concentrated pointedly on the family, on Juno, on the changing nature of personal relationships under stress, Odets fuzzed the issues by dividing our attention between Bessie and the inner worlds of her family on the one hand, and the Depression, the outer world, on the other.

The men in *Awake and Sing* puzzle us. Impotent (they have no jobs, no money), they blame the world, a vague outside force, in an almost classical displacement of responsibility. How seriously are we to take their social sense when we discover that Bessie's father, the "intellectual" radical, has not even cut the pages of the revolutionary books he passes on to Ralphie as a legacy? We hope that Ralphie will be released from his imprisonment by the suicide of his grandfather. For Ralphie, like his father and grandfather, is more the victim of his mother than of the Depression. But he does not see anything of the sort. His unfocused aggression is sporadic; he never fully releases his violence; he cannot name his actual jailer; but he is struggling toward honesty and does not readily fool himself by attacking a scapegoat.

Awake and Sing, of course, has the outlines and a good deal of the substance of tragedy. But the characters are too easily absolved of responsibility for their action (and inaction) by the Depression. If men are indeed directed by economic forces, as Brecht indicated, we should see this clearly and directly, not ambiguously. Is Bessie's husband a shadow of a man because of economics or because of his own inadequacy (determined by any combination of nonsocial and social factors)? Does Bessie's father commit suicide because he is escaping from a finally intolerable family situation, or because he wants to help his family, or because he has no job as a barber? Is Bessie's daughter beaten into defeat by the nature of human life itself or by the specific, limited outside world of the Depression?

Odets is perhaps unfairly assessed in relation to Brecht. The genius of Odets is in his capacity for poetry; his plays come alive and compel us whatever the confusion in their making. Odets is to be compared with writers of the order of Shakespeare, whose art surpassed their mere understanding. It seems true, to be sure, that Odets, without the generating force of the Depression, of the Social Problem, allowed his genius to subside; his Hollywood work was merely intelligent contrivance.

It is Arthur Miller who demands a close and fair comparison with Brecht, for it is in Miller's social plays that we see the plain attempt to transcend the particular and achieve the universal, to create a Tragedy of Modern Man, as Miller himself and some critics have put it. *All My Sons* is intended as an epic in miniature of the corrupting effect of "dog eat dog" capitalist society: a shallow, callous, brutal small businessman destroys himself and his family merely by adhering to what seem to be the rules of his society. *Death of a Salesman* is the epic of the low man in our society, how he is hoodwinked by it, and finally—again —destroyed by it. *The Crucible* is to be read as a kind of universal account of the powers of evil, those that

depend on false accusation and persecution of innocent men.

Death of a Salesman, more than *The Crucible*,
provides the challenge, for it is persuasive both in its
smaller and larger dimensions. In spite of the occasional references to brand-name items, it seems
intended as allegory: the hero is Everyman, and is
actually named "Low Man," Willy Loman; he is a
Salesman, selling himself and not any particular product; he moves through space and time at will with little
relation to reality (as Robert Warshow in *The Immediate Experience* put it, he seems trapped like a rat in
the gigantic maze of the setting right on the stage);
his human needs are rejected in the presence of a tape
recorder; his sons have names of types, "Biff" and
"Happy." The death is not the death of a Jewish
salesman with a Jewish family, of someone who comes
out of the highly particularized world of Odets; it is
the death of any American salesman, of any person
who sells and has allowed himself to be sold on "the
American dream."

But Willy Loman is not only an allegorical figure;
he is also made sufficiently an individual that we must
pause to wonder just how much personal responsibility he bears for his fate. What ruins his son? We
have two possibilities: the empty dream of easy heroic
glory on the football field, the glory that is merely
physical, in the accident of muscle and athletic power
(Irwin Shaw has a short story whose unsuccessful hero,
also a football player, is named Christian Darling,
or, on application forms, last name first, Darling
Christian: the archetypal American hero of the
golden twenties). The second possibility to account
for Biff's failure has nothing to do with generaliza-
tion: the son discovered the father in a hotel room
with Another Woman. If we are to consider the first

possibility seriously, we are asked to accept the easily disprovable proposition that football players in the American nature of things cannot turn out well, can never become Supreme Court justices, for example. If we accept the second, we have a different proposition altogether, one that belongs in an O'Neill play perhaps, and perhaps not there either, for the world is more real in O'Neill than for a son to become a waster simply on discovering that his father is an adulterer (see *Long Day's Journey into Night*).

Truth in Brecht is plainly a different matter from that in Ibsen. Brecht's truth is that of large caricature (caricature that magnifies not shrinks), of epic, of Michelangelo, of abstract sculpture or painting. Universality in art may come, to be sure, as the particular begins to illuminate, to become, the general; but universality may start in universality, that is, it may begin with abstracted forms; it may leap away at once from possibility and actuality to the realm of comprehensible distortion and fantasy. With Brecht, we are only part way toward the totally abstract landscape of Beckett, but we are equally far removed from the drawing rooms, people, towns of Ibsen, which have locations in time and place.

Miller would seem to want it both ways, both as art and as document, as a sort of hedge against being misunderstood for saying too little or too much. Loman is both Salesman and salesman and is consequently neither completely. The question as to what he carries in his valises is a fair one only if we fail to see that allegorically it does not matter what Willy sells, but we cannot easily allow ourselves to drop this question, for we are gratuitously given answers to so many similar small questions we would not even bother asking. Miller persuades us of the smaller authenticities about the Lomans and their fate while hoping that we will be carried away into accepting them as personages, as "paradigms," who transcend their immediacy and become tragic. And we are very nearly compelled by the enormous skill of the play to accept them so. This is skillful propaganda but it is not art, for art will survive any challenges. The massive authenticity of Brecht is lacking.

Miller has not written about the Rosenbergs per se, or about Hiss and Chambers, or about an actual salesman or small manufacturer, for his ambition is to say something Big. Yet he will not say anything big directly, as Brecht did, for then he must transcend ideology, so to speak, as Brecht did; he must get down to the actuality of thought and idea and not, as Robert Warshow put it, the appearance or the gesture of thought. If *The Crucible* is to justify its universal import, it must apply with equal validity to all trials based on insane accusations, to the trials of the Inquisition as well as to the Moscow trials of the late thirties (which is an inconvenience). It must also evoke Kafka's *Trial*, which is the classical literary instance of a trial without sense, and even remind us of the trying of Job, whose trial made a theological or existential sense only. We cannot think of a symbolic, a literary trial today without at once hearing a whole chamber of reverberating echoes. But while Miller may well want us, to judge from the text, to think of the Salem witch trials as embodying all injustice or insane justice in human history, he really preferred us to think of his play, at least when it was first written and produced, as limiting its comment to contemporary "witch hunts" of Communists who are not Communists.

Brecht, Hellman, Odets, and Miller were involved, one way or another, in the leftist movements of our time. Politics cannot easily be omitted in any discussion of their work although, obviously, politics cannot explain esthetic matters. Politics does explain choice of subject, however, and even avoidance of it, and the combination of politics and the man may even help account for some aspect of esthetic success.

Thus, Brecht and Odets always transcended their material—and their politics. Odets's leftist ideology is a minor thread, finally, in the vastly rich total fabric of his plays; *Awake and Sing*, like *Juno and the Paycock*, rises above any of the specific revolutionary themes so as to reside on another level of discussion altogether. The Depression in Odets and the Rebellion in O'Casey are powerful motivating forces, both of situation and theme, but they are, in a way, general irritants rather than specific ones; they may even, conceivably, be abstracted into the general pressures of living itself.

Brecht and Odets, too, in their entirely different ways of course, had no hesitation in naming names. Jews as Jews, for example, appear in both, but not in the plays of Miller. Both Brecht and Odets, again differently, accepted the forces of the particular. Miller has repeatedly universalized, in spite of the fact that most members of the audience on Broadway that saw *Death of a Salesman* must have supposed that the characters were Jewish, and some of those that saw *The Crucible* must have thought of the Rosenbergs in relation to the Proctors.

If we are to get hold of any idea at all in a play, as Lionel Abel has remarked, we must be able to become the characters, to share their impulses and values, for at least some instant. We must want the same things they do. We obviously do not need their pedigrees to believe in characters; we believe in Everyman. We do not need tape-recorded naturalness in speech, motion-picture caught eccentricity of behavior, to be made to believe; we'll believe in the dancelike movements of the people in Lorca, in the puppetlike ones of those in Beckett, in the grand, larger-than-life ones of those in Brecht.

But to believe without a nagging and a corroding doubt, we must accept the idea of the play, we must respond to its moral thrust. Brecht's first concern, much like that of Shaw's, was in "teaching." Brecht brought to his teaching a sense of theater, however, more like that of Pirandello than that of Shaw, although Shaw, too, did not deceive himself about the unreality of the medium. For Brecht, the theater was not a place to convey a sense merely of some portion of life outside, to reproduce reality, whether in terms of atmosphere or of fidelity to facts (time, place, historical movements) or of psychological accuracy. The stage for Brecht was landscape itself where the playwright, aided by the usual team of theatrical artists, could range panoramically in time and space. He sought to "alienate" his audience, to make it rise out of passivity and placidity. His idea, his substance, his intention was idea, idea as it has its origins and dynamics in the wide world and in all time. Ideology, commitment to a system that arranges idea, was obviously always present in Brecht. But it was attenuated, finally lost, as Abel among others shows, as ideology embodied itself in character, setting, situation, became, finally, idea itself. This almost happens in Odets, as his characters achieve their own life, make their own way, nearly disentangle themselves from ideology. It does not happen in Hellman's or in Miller's social plays: ideology remains unassimilated. If it sinks out of view, it still adulterates.

We cannot fairly ask the same ingenuous questions of Brecht we ask of Miller and Hellman (and sometimes of Odets), having to do with the emperor's clothes. Brecht does not *pretend* to give us an emperor, does not *pretend* to adorn him with clothes; his emperors are clearly not emperors and are clearly naked. For all of their quality of caricature and fantasy, we are not puzzled by Joan of the stockyards, by the good woman of Setzuan, by Galileo, as we are by Willy Loman, by Regina, by Ralphie. Brecht's figures are out of epic, and we accept them as we accept the crafty Ulysses, the petulant Achilles, the brave Hector; we have been prepared by Brecht to see them on this larger stage, engaged in this larger, symbolic activity. The characters of Hellman, Miller, and often of Odets are out of some small formula for making propaganda plays (the power of Bessie in *Awake and Sing* arises from the playwright's incapacity to fit her into formula).

Brecht, of course, was European, which is to say, among other things, that politics was not the dominating force for him that it has been for American party-line radicals. Picasso continues to turn out works of the sort described in Moscow as decadent. A commitment to revolutionary political doctrine does not keep the European intellectual, as it seems to keep the American, from a free, widely ranging use of his genius. American social artists often become simply doctrinaire, using art in behalf of propaganda. They will go so far, as Odets did in *Waiting for Lefty* (with ingenious success), as to have an audience join in the action at the curtain by rising and, with clenched fists, shouting "Strike! Strike!" O'Casey made some of his revolutionary heroes humanly shallow, without thereby denying the validity of the revolution. In Europe, a revolution is greater than its makers.

Brecht's moral involvement with his subject matter kept him from blunting the quality of his people with the pettiness of documentation or the ballooning of grandiosity. His characters do not have to stop and tell us who they are and what they are and why (as the mother in *All My Sons* tells everyone that she knows all about herself, or as Kurt Müller explains to Brancovis how innocent Americans are, or as Ralph talks about awaking and singing). We learn what sort of world Brecht's people live in, and what sort of people they are, from seeing it and them in a created context.

Epic theater is precisely what Brecht created: Homer and Sophocles and Aeschylus and Euripides certainly tell us more of the Greek world than do statistical, archeological, historical details (although the latter of course do tell us much, just as Odets, Miller, and Hellman tell us much about the social phenomena of the thirties, forties, and fifties in varying degrees and in different ways). We get the *idea* of the Greeks from Homer; we get the *idea* of contemporary Western man from Brecht. We get this idea without equivocation, without pomposity, without dogma, without sentimentality, in Brecht.

THE DRAMA of social protest, or simply of social criticism, from Ibsen and Shaw through Brecht to the party-line playwrights of the thirties, embodied an anger that was specifically directed. It implied a promise: if this or that social problem were eliminated, the anger would subside. Comes the revolution, Ralphie Berger would awake and sing; the Hubbards, the little foxes that spoil the vines, would be liquidated. In *Death of a Salesman*, we may assume that some sort of company "security" plan, augmented by appropriate state arrangements, would have kept Willy Loman from descending into his state of hopeless economic deprivation, or at least would have mitigated the hopelessness; some form of family or personal counselling might have salvaged his domestic and personal dignity.

In *A Streetcar Named Desire*, by contrast, Kowalski is firmly and contentedly established in a social arrangement; his anger has no social content or end. Indeed, he is engaged in continually separating himself from the dominant bourgeois amenities and decencies of society while simultaneously asserting their importance: he is outraged to find his best friend being inveigled into a respectable relationship, marriage, with a prostitute. Yet, he is physically filthy, by virtue of his job *and* his inclination: his dirtiness is the consequence of an undirected anger, a never subdued inner violence, that explodes whimsically, even at his closest friends, his poker companions. His anger, his temper, his deliberate disorder, establish his relation to society: he gives himself an individuality through unpredictability, muscular assertiveness, a mumbling parody of clear speech, a defiant and pietistic pride in belonging to the class of grease-stained, unwashed, Ku Klux Klan platoon sergeants of American life.

Jimmie Porter, in Osborne's *Look Back in Anger*, well-educated, is no more focussed in his anger although he is more articulate. He attacks, insults, derides any form of establishmentarianism. Society's awfulness simply cannot be handled by individual and small palliatives. He withdraws from civilization to a personal and private world, reverting to infantile antics, hopping about like a teddy bear. For a period, he lapses into domestic placidity, with his mistress, but he must return to his wife, to the socially approved situation, which provides a more meaningful context both for his verbal and physical sadistic brutalities, more meaningful because he is more involved, socially and emotionally, and for his detachment from the meaningless rat-climbing of *Room at the Top* and of some of Kingsley Amis' characters.

Both Porter and Kowalski find themselves in claustrophobic domestic situations; parallels between the two plays may be worked out, perhaps with more plausibility than validity. The significant difference is that Porter makes only the barest gesture of accommodation to the establishment; Kowalski accepts it as a given, defies it, yet supports its simplest-minded values. Where Kowalski might join the Ku Klux Klan, Porter would join a trade union or the Labour Party. But I think the point is that Porter, at least while we see him, can join nothing that has ties with a larger social world that has ties with Buchenwald and Hiroshima that has ties with the organized total world of governments and politics. Porter's anger, especially in its sheerly sadistic moments (which should never be separated from the enormous, pure childlike sympathy he is capable of), is directed against the awful possibilities in humanity itself, in himself.

Camus's *Caligula*, who pushes his sadism to extreme possibilities, similarly encapsulates an anger that reaches proportions of heroism: he quite hopelessly dares mankind, men, himself, to make him other than he is. Unapologetic, that is, not looking for or contriving some philosophical sophistry as de Sade kept doing to justify himself, he tries repeatedly to unjustify himself, to find proof that he cannot be Venus, that he cannot continue to be Caligula. Caligula creates absurdity after absurdity in the game of stretching the tightrope he walks as tautly fine as it can be made just short of breaking. Anger in its various extremes of distortion, vengefulness, whimsical sadism, instinctive self-defense, masochistic self-denial, blind cleverness of mind and tongue make the context of Caligula's world—by his will. He makes the system of madness the only sanity. He evokes Bernarda Alba or Gregers Werle.

Madness and fantasy, the methodical enlargement of absurdity, continue to emerge in modern drama as ways of confronting the arrangements of civilization, the outrageous ones as well as the ordinary ones, of engaging with and accommodating to them. *The Madwoman of Chaillot* deliberately cultivates a personal whimsicality into a style of carriage for meeting daily challenges, large and small: choosing one's clothes, comforting a suicide, dealing with a combine of speculators, having an interlude for a social tea, supporting the innocence and frailty of young love. Two opposing groups emerge to play at surviving: the uncivilized representatives of "civilization"; the civilized exiles from that "civilization."

In *The Visit*, Duerrenmatt has his fabulously rich heroine put the issue succinctly: "The world has made me a prostitute, and I am making it a brothel." Genet, most specifically in *The Balcony*, obliquely in *The Blacks*, describes the ritualistic fantasies, the straining after implausible possibilities, that mark a passage through the brothel of the world. The underworld in Giraudoux is brought to the surface: "Why this is hell, nor are we out of it."

The anger of these plays simply expunges the world, negates it: it is *not* that familiar and ordered arrangement of values and activities we are comfortably familiar with: it is a Hieronymus Bosch landscape jumbled with the abominably persuasive, grotesque, mechanical monsters, modified for the present by Dali, de Chirico, Giacometti, Picasso, Francis Bacon.

Anger in Anouilh's *Antigone* is set in the social and political context of the extremities of tyranny. The excessively rational madness of tyranny, of Creon-Hitler-Stalin, opposes the impulsive whimsicality of the personal and private. Creon and Antigone are compelled by a suppressed anger that carries them to the abyss of an absurd self-destruction that is simultaneously self-identifying: they uncover the worst and best in themselves. Creon begs his victim to have pity on him, to spare him from the momentum of the machine of power he himself set into motion. It is Antigone who may seem at moments willfully cruel, in asserting so absolutely her inflexible whim to resist the dynamo of law, order, society. Creon's reasonableness, his facts, his seeming sense of control are defensive, inadequately so in the end. They do not finally defend him or his son or his niece. The *merely*, frivolously, pointlessly human has a power to subdue the logically riveted, welded arrangements, the vanities of an ambition that seeks to extend and enlarge the plain human out of its instinctive propriety, decency, and sheer vulnerability of flesh, bone, blood, and nerve.

The essences of private and social human experience, abstracted from history, are delineated in Beckett's *Waiting for Godot,* where place and time and plot are made irrelevant. One might start the play at the end as easily as at the beginning or in the middle; if the play has any determinable scheme it is that of a dream. Arguments, tensions, rapprochements in the play have no content, only form. The relationships are abstractly fraternal or paternal; they are strained to their limits; the characters live by performing and commenting on this, as in Pirandello. The strained conversation to create a social setting is like that in Ionesco's *The Bald Soprano.* Anger is stimulated deliberately and emptily as a way of creating a moment of vitality. The reductive childlike interdependence of the pairs of characters emphasizes how essential is the most primitive rapport between humans to achieve some moment, some semblance of emotional aliveness in the vast lunar emptiness of endless living.

The absurd, as has been contended, is not new in drama. Absurdities, illogicalities, implausibilities, fantasies may be found in every period of the theater. Indeed, the absurd may be seen as merely a logical extension of the absurdity of theatricality itself, as a *reductio ad absurdum,* so to speak.

But the "absurd" in the most recent theater has an altogether different intention from "absurdity." We can find instances of the absurd in Shaw, Wilde, and Pirandello if we choose to think of the absurd simply as absurdity. Mrs. Warren, chairman of the board of an international cartel of brothels, is an absurd caricature of a prostitute risen to madame; the grossness of the absurdity is a measure of Shaw's angry attack on poverty. She is like one of Gropper's ugly fat "capitalists." Lear's ridiculous egotism, his absurd defiance of the forces of mortality, is turned at the end into a calm, bland sanity, as he descends from his insane heights of blasting the very heavens. The absurd dance of attendance which Wilde's heroes perform before their petty gods reflects the narrow, refined, furtive madness of Wilde's society. Pirandello's absurdities have as their immediate point the interrelatedness of the theatrical with the real, the effect that drama can have on the large audience surrounding the stage, the reciprocal effect that that large audience can have on the stage.

The modern absurd, however, as distinguished from absurdity, or absurd details, is more narrowly focused, to make a direct, sometimes small, often diamond-hard moral point. The technique of the modern absurd does not *serve*, is not subordinated to, philosophical or social intentions (which themselves, of course, might well ultimately be moral). The modern absurd becomes one with the moral. As in modern art, the canvas, the material for sculpture, become the art itself, not referrents to *other*, removed ideas or objects.

Ionesco's middle-class English evening, *The Bald Soprano*, is immediately absurd, absurd on the surface, not through details of plot or character. The absurd in Chekhov comes to us through the complexities and shades of character of Lyubov Andreyevna and her brother; of the obsessiveness of an Arkadina or of an Ivanov. It is the implausible glitter of conversation in Wilde which is absurd. In Ionesco we have no plot, little characterization, sometimes none. We have directly that one-dimensional surface which in modern painting is itself. The surrealistic touching up here and there of the canvas forces an additional concentration on the thing as it itself is. The events and persons in *The Bald Soprano* can be nothing else but themselves, two typical English couples literally engaged in the acting out of nothing, nothing at all, except themselves; we find no shadings of character; there is no involvement with one another or with other events. The Fire Chief, who might conceivably have provoked an engagement with something outside that evening, that room, turns out himself to be looking for a fire, for that thing to do which defines him. He gradually loses his dimensionality in that flat drawing room. He is as disengaged as the Smiths and the Martins.

The character in *The New Tenant* has no identity outside his involvement with the things which engulf him. The victims of duty, in the play with that title, are just that, nothing else, carrying out some excessive, puritanical cleansing out of depths.

Amédée has something of a plot, namely, the problem of "how to get rid of it," the corpse, that is, of his wife's former lover. But it is determinedly fantasticated away from the real and toward the sur-real, the more than real, and consequently unrepresentational: the mushrooms that keep sprouting; the corpse that keeps growing and finally balloons away; the telephone switchboard in the living room; the play that can't get written by Amédée beyond the one line he has set down.

In all of these, Ionesco shows flatly alienated, baffled, bored, empty, impotent, modern men as they are just these: alienated, baffled, empty, impotent. His characters rarely achieve any independent identity that takes them away from ourselves (except here and there; Amédée certainly rouses our sympathy, but it comes from identification of him with the funny little man in derby, baggy pants, and ill-fitting shoes).

We cannot particularize the place or time in Ionesco, and, paradoxically, we cannot absolve ourselves of involvement: Shaw's world, after all, is not our world, and we can readily shrug away the conditions that created the outrageous rationalizations of a Mrs. Warren or an Andrew Undershaft; Wilde's world ended with the gradual disintegration of British social boundaries; Chekhov's, with Lenin's revolution. In Ionesco, we become his characters: we join his inane English couples, whose evenings start as they begin, that hellish present doom Sartre depicts in *No Exit*.

Ionesco's *Rhinoceros* may be said to be less successful than his other work precisely because it becomes too allegorical, too related to events and people that have identity. It succeeds most when an actor like Zero Mostel or Laurence Olivier can transcend the play, that is, rise out of the immediacy of character and plot to become as independent as the new tenant, or as Mr. and Mrs. Smith, to become a rhinoceros or the archetypal Chaplin.

The absurd in Ionesco works its effect by thrusting itself on us directly: the dreams are our dreams; the tape-recorded flatness of idle talk, our talk; the wild, oppressive guilts, our own guilts stripped of any social or historical insulation. Recognition, identification, confession, are forced directly upon us.

Albee, too, eliminates some of the traditional insulating, protecting techniques of the drama. He takes the truth implicit in a situation to its inevitable and consequently, always, absurd conclusion: the grandma burying herself, the casual park pickup that ends in murder, the Pop Art embodiment of the American dream (that muscular yet impotent statue combining Atlas and Joe Palooka), the domestic fun-and-games that concludes with a churchlike ritual. His plays are sometimes simple onslaughts, as Antonin Artaud suggested drama should be, as The Living Theatre's production of *The Brig* was. A smoldering anger provides a sub-surface of vitality in Albee, becoming absurdly nondirected, free-floating as it rises into the surface action.

The small absurdities in Albee—like the lady caller who strips to her slip on the invitation to make herself comfortable—should not obscure the larger ones, which have a different quality and dimension. In *The American Dream*, the area of the absurd that speaks directly to us—and not simply because it is logically macabre yet familiar—is the description of the parental dismemberment of the infant that played with its private parts. In *The Zoo Story*, the absurd manifests itself in the sudden ambiguous suicide-murder; in the *Sandbox*, it comes from grandma's acting out in so many gestures the exact meaning of her family's attitude toward her, as she buries herself in sand. Each absurdity is rooted in anger.

The mysterious son of the older couple in *Who's Afraid of Virginia Woolf?*, as well as the conclusion of the play, that mock ceremonial combination of awe and derision present in the black mass, suggest Ionesco's use of the absurd as direct communication, without the intention of code or symbol, let alone conventional "plot." The intensity of response toward their "son" (we must speak of him in quotation marks, for the text plainly suggests that even if he exists literally, he has other than merely filial meaning) is evidence of their "need" for him, whether this need is parental or merely domestic. The son, then, becomes that force inherent in any private bond that husbands and wives evolve. The disintegration of that shared bond becomes, like the splitting of the atom, the dissolution of the marriage, the innermost nucleus of the marriage being exposed first, then exploded. After the fissionable materials have reached their critical mass, we come to the climax of ritual antimarriage; we find ourselves reverting to the antisacramental nature involved in mutual destruction. Even if the marriage survives, it will have undergone an alchemical change.

Albee "absurdly" carries out the domestic horrors implicit in Strindberg and in O'Neill. Both Strindberg and O'Neill hinted at possibilities which Albee fulfills in good measure: the masks in *Marco Millions,* the alternating familial attacks and sheltering of *Long Day's Journey into Night;* the stark descent to madness in *The Father,* the repetitive, balletlike vignettes of *A Dream Play. The Zoo Story* moves relentlessly toward its black finale like *Miss Julie.*

Where Ionesco may be said to be working with the social absurd, Albee works with the psychological absurd. Ionesco follows through on the thrust implicit in Brecht (pace his famous quarrel with him), and Albee on that implicit in Strindberg and O'Neill. The absurd eliminates from their work the possibility that even a shred of detachment may remain, as we seek refuge in the logic and explanation of plot, place, characterization, biography, theatrical history, production technicalities.

That directness of statement, so characteristic in the modern theater of that persuasively reasonable extravagance we find in any bold art, is perhaps most cogently to be examined in Pinter, whose *The Caretaker* actually has no "fantasy" in it at all, in the sense of some distortion of reality, and whose *The Dumbwaiter* does not really depend for its effect on its fantastic elements.

Pinter offers the temptation to begin a number of literary analogies. There is much in him that is similar to Beckett; a number of details evoke Eliot's "Sweeney Agonistes." John Russell Brown, in a brilliant, compact essay, has related Pinter to Shakespeare. The absurd universe of Chaplin, Keaton, Laurel and Hardy, even of Harold Lloyd, is the tone of much of Pinter, the slapstick cleared of the merely incongruous; the pies that get thrown, free of the whipped topping; the effect, when it is successful, as in Chaplin principally, is that of tragicomedy.

Unlike Beckett's landscape, which is lunar and timeless, Pinter's is all too-worldly and immediate; his settings have the cluttered thinginess of slum rooms. *The Dumbwaiter* begins with a dumb show reminiscent not only of some of the exchanges in *Waiting for Godot* but in a Laurel and Hardy skit. Gus and Ben are not so much looking for something to do, to complain about, in order to find a dialogue to make union, as they are caught up in some momentary nuisance of daily life. Professional executioners, they are partners —like the killers in the Hemingway story—used to working and living together, waiting for an assignment, excluding all other activity in the world from anything but their most passing scrutiny. They become maniacally engaged in satisfying the needs of the dumbwaiter, presumably feeding some Ionesco-like restaurant upstairs, in order to preserve their exclusive identity as killers waiting to be set into action. Finally, their mission turns against themselves (it hardly matters, from this point of view, who kills whom in the end).

The Caretaker is an exercise in the pathology of the ordinary. The characters of *Waiting for Godot* are taken out of a landscape designed for them by a Dali or a di Chirico and set into one that looks as though it might have just been abandoned by a company doing

Gorky's *The Lower Depths*. The dialogue rarely achieves even the sick vitality of gallows humor.

In writing of Gelber's *The Connection*, Lionel Abel in *Metatheatre* has remarked that the audience is caught up in the pointless, anticlimactic waiting of the play itself: the audience's waiting for a "plot," for conflict, for resolution, for climax is like the waiting of the characters for their "connection." Gelber, of course, pretends he has no play, just "happenings" overflowing the stage into the audience and out into the lobby and the street outside. Pinter keeps his action strictly behind the footlights, but the aimless, frequently clinical exactness of the talk forces us to be present as we watch clownlike characters grasp at finding meaning, making contact, in their pointless private activity—going to sleep, waking up, groping in the dark, muttering self-deluding myths of identification or ambition. The familiarly clinical becomes *theatrically* absurd.

Paradoxically, the question of the ordinary in Genet is beside the point. It is his contempt and anger, the merciless brutality of his truths, which give his works their defining quality. The absurd in Genet is subordinate to his angry essaylike explorations; it is his anger that raises his absurd charades into theatrical rituals that force audiences to participate against their will and reason. And it is Genet, perhaps, in blending anger and absurdity, or, rather, transmuting the first into the second, who makes most penetrating the moral point of absurdity. Social or personal *logic*, by contrast, becomes a negation of the happiest human possibility.

The absurd as a moral force is the dominant poetic in the works of Genet, Beckett, Ionesco, Pinter, and Albee. The moral impulse generated in the modern theater by Ibsen, given momentum in their various ways by Strindberg, Chekhov, Shaw, and Pirandello, does not make for an easy, unambiguously intentioned drama, where all things are plainly what they are. It encourages mysteries of contradictions, shadings, and depths, but it celebrates, finally, the richness and the rightness of the human condition, which must always be made better and, hopefully, kept so through examinations of every kind.

NHTI-FARNUM LIBRARY

a3466200158038a

PN
1851   Freedman
.F7   The moral impulse

Date Due

Printed in U.S.A.